THE RESURRECTION FACTOR

by

JOSH McDOWELL

HERE'S LIFE PUBLISHERS, INC.
San Bernardino, California 92402

THE RESURRECTION FACTOR

A Campus Crusade for Christ Book

Published by
HERE'S LIFE PUBLISHERS, INC.
P.O. Box 1576
San Bernardino, Calif. 92402

ISBN 0-918956-72-2
HLP Product No. 40-279-2

Library of Congress Catalogue Card 80-71049
Copyright © 1981 Campus Crusade for Christ, Inc.
All rights reserved.

Manufactured in the United States of America.

To the staff of The Julian Center whose vision and commitment are for The Resurrection Factor experience to be a reality in the lives of all those who come to study with us.

Contents

CHAPTER ONE

THE
<u>STRUGGLE</u>

> *"I have had few difficulties, many friends, great successes; I have gone from wife to wife, and from house to house, visited great countries of the world, but I am fed up with inventing devices to fill up 24 hours of the day."*
>
> (Suicide Note)
> **Ralph Barton**
> *Cartoonist*

> *"I sit in my house in Buffalo and sometimes I get so lonely it's unbelievable. Life has been so good to me. I've got a great wife, good kids, money, my own health — and I'm lonely and bored. . . . I often wondered why so many rich people commit suicide. Money sure isn't a cure-all."*
>
> **O.J. Simpson**
> *Football Super-Star*
> *Millionaire*
> *(People Magazine, June 12, 1978)*

Why is it that three simple questions cast an eerie silence across almost any university audience in America? It happens whenever I ask: "Who are you? Why in the world are you here? Where are you going?"

THE SEARCH BEGINS

As a university student, I couldn't answer those questions. Maybe you can't either. But I wanted to. Like everyone else I wanted meaning in life. I wanted to be happy. I wanted to be the happiest individual in the world. And what could be wrong with that as long as my happiness wasn't at the expense of someone else?

Happiness

Not long ago, I was riding double on a motorcycle with a friend of mine in Newport Beach, Calif. We were talking, laughing and having a good time. I enjoy life. In fact, it's one reason my doctor tells me I'll never get ulcers — I laugh a lot and tell people exactly what I think.

As we were riding along, two women pulled alongside us in a new Lincoln Continental. For two blocks, at 20 miles an hour, they just stared at us. Finally the lady on the passenger side rolled down her window. "What right do you have to be so happy?" she yelled out. Before we could reply, she rolled up her window and they sped away. But the answer to her question is simple: I want to be happy and I've found the source.

Freedom

More than that I want to be free. I want to be one of the freest individuals in the world. Freedom to me is not going out and doing whatever I wish. Anyone can do that. And lots of people are. <u>Freedom is possessing the power to do what I know I ought to do</u>. By that definition, most people aren't free. They know what they ought to do, but they don't have the power to do it. They're in bondage. And as a university student, so was I.

The Struggle

Religion

I started looking for answers. Almost everyone it seems is into some sort of religion, so I took off for church. I went in the morning. I went in the afternoon. I went in the evening. But I must have found the wrong church. I felt worse inside than I did outside.

Being a practical sort of person, I chuck anything that doesn't work. So I chucked religion. The only thing I ever got out of religion was the 25 cents I put in the offering — and the 35 cents I took out for a milkshake.

But that's more than many people ever gain from "religion," I reassured myself, and no matter what the pastor said, I still believed in God.

Prestige

I began to wonder, could prestige be the answer? Perhaps being a leader, adopting some cause, giving myself to it, and "being known" might do it.

At the first university I attended, the student leaders held the purse strings and threw their weight around. So I ran for freshman class president and was elected.

It was neat making the decisions, spending the students' and university's money to get speakers I wanted, knowing everyone on campus, and having everyone say, "Hi, Josh." But, as with everything else I had tried, the glamor wore off. I would wake up Monday morning (usually with a headache from the night before), and my attitude would be, "Well, here goes another five days." I simply endured Monday through Friday. Happiness revolved around three nights: Friday, Saturday and Sunday. It was a vicious circle.

Frustration

Oh, I fooled them at the university. Everyone thought I was one of the most happy-go-lucky guys around. The phrase on my political campaign buttons was, "Happiness Is Josh." I threw more parties with student money than anyone else. But my happiness was like so many other people's: It depended on my own circumstances. If things were going great, I felt great. When things would go lousy, I felt lousy.

I was like a boat in the ocean, tossed about by waves of circumstances. Everyone around me was living the same way. The faculty could tell me how to make a better living, but they couldn't tell me how to live better. Everyone could tell me what I ought to do, but none could give me the power to do it.

The world

Frustration began to plague me.

THE STRUGGLE CONTINUES

Few people in the universities and colleges of this country were ever more sincere than I in trying to find meaning, truth and purpose to life. Try as I might, these goals eluded me.

It was about this time I noticed a small group of people at the university — eight students and two faculty members. There was something different about their lives. They seemed to know *why* they believed what they believed.

I like to be around people like that. I don't care if people don't agree with *me*. Some of my closest friends are opposed to some things I believe. But I admire a man or woman with conviction. (Maybe that's because there are so few of them.) Contrary to most other university students, the people in this small group seemed to know where they were going.

Love demonstrated

These people also didn't just *talk* about love. They got involved. They seemed to be riding above the circumstances of university life, when everybody else appeared to be under those circumstances. Then, too, I noticed their happiness. They appeared to possess a constant, inner source of joy. In fact, they were disgustingly happy. Obviously, they had something I didn't.

And like the average student, when somebody had something I didn't have, I wanted it. That's why you have to lock up your bicycle on the college campus. Someone may want it. <u>If education were really the answer, the university probably would be the most morally upright community in existence. But it's not</u>.

I wanted what I saw, so I decided to make friends with these intriguing people.

Two weeks later, we were all sitting around a table in the student union: six students and two faculty members. The conversation started to swing to God. Now, if you're insecure, and a conversation begins to center on God, you tend to put on a big front. On every campus, in every community, in every office, there's always "the big mouth," a person who says, "Uh . . . Christianity, ha ha. That's for weaklings, it's not intellectual." (Usually, the bigger the mouth, the greater the insecurity.)

The challenge

The conversation began to bother me. Finally I looked over at one of the students, a good-looking woman (I used to think all Christians were ugly). Leaning back in my chair (I didn't want the others to think I was too interested), I said, "Tell me, what changed your life? Why is yours so different from the other students, the leaders on this campus, the professors?"

That young woman must have had a lot of conviction. She looked me straight in the eye and, with a little smile, said two words I never thought I'd hear in a university as part of a solution.

"Jesus Christ," she said.

"Oh, for heaven's sake, don't give me that garbage about religion," I said.

She shot back, "Mister, I didn't say religion; I said Jesus Christ."

Right there she pointed out something I'd never known before. Christianity is not a religion. Religion may be defined as humans trying to work their way to God through good works. Christianity, on the other hand, is God coming to men and women through Jesus Christ, offering them a relationship with Himself.

There probably are more people with misconceptions about Christianity in universities than anywhere else in society. Recently, in a graduate seminar, I met a teaching assistant who remarked, "Anyone who walks into a church becomes a Christian."

"Does walking into a garage make you a car?" I replied.

There is no correlation. One becomes a Christian only by putting his trust in Christ.

My new friends challenged me intellectually to examine the claims that Jesus Christ is God's Son; that taking on human flesh He lived among real men and women and died on the cross for the sins of mankind; that He was buried and He arose three days later and could change a person's life in the 20th century.

Intellectual suicide

I thought it was a farce. In fact, I thought most Christians were walking idiots. I'd met some. I used to wait for a Christian to speak up in the classroom so I could beat the professor to the punch in tearing him or her up one side and down the other. I thought that if a Christian had a brain cell, it would die of loneliness. I didn't know any better.

But these people challenged me over and over. Finally, I accepted. But I did it out of pride, to refute them. I didn't know there were facts. I didn't know there was evidence a person could evaluate with his mind.

After much study and research, my mind finally came to the conclusion that Jesus Christ must have been who He claimed to be. In fact, my search to refute Christianity became the background behind my first two books. When I couldn't refute it, I ended up becoming a Christian. I now have spent 13 years documenting why I believe that faith in Jesus Christ is intellectually feasible.

One of the crucial areas of my research to refute Christianity centered around the resurrection.

A student at the University of Uruguay said to me: "Professor McDowell, why can't you intellectually refute Christianity?"

"For a very simple reason," I answered. "I am not able to explain away an event in history — the resurrection of Jesus Christ."

After more than 1,000 hours of studying this subject and thoroughly investigating its foundation, I was forced to the conclusion that the resurrection of Jesus Christ is either one of the most wicked, heartless, vicious, hoaxes ever foisted upon the minds of men, or it is the most fantastic fact of history. It is either history's greatest delusion or the greatest miracle that history records.

The crucial issue

The resurrection issue removes the question, "Is Christianity valid?" from the realm of philosophy and forces it to be an issue of history.

Does Christianity have an historically acceptable basis?

Does sufficient evidence exist to warrant belief in the resurrection?

Some of the facts relevant to the resurrection are these: Jesus of Nazareth, a Jewish prophet, claimed to be the Christ prophesied in the Jewish Scriptures. He was arrested, judged a political criminal, and crucified. Three days after His death and burial, some women went to His tomb and found the body gone. His disciples claimed that God had raised Him from the dead and that He had appeared to them various times before ascending into heaven.

From this foundation, Christianity spread throughout the Roman Empire and has continued to exert great influence down through the centuries.

Did the resurrection actually happen? Was the tomb of Jesus really empty? The controversy over these questions rages even today.

Summary

In college I was a student leader . . . in a frustrated search like everyone else for the true source of happiness and freedom. I encountered a small group of students and faculty who claimed that Jesus Christ had changed their lives. I listened only because they demonstrated the love about which they talked. As a skeptic I accepted their challenge to examine intellectually the claims that Jesus Christ was God's Son, that He was buried and arose three days later, and that He can change a person's life in the twentieth century.

Surprisingly, I couldn't refute Christianity because I couldn't explain away one crucial event in history — the resurrection of Jesus Christ. I became a believer. This book documents what I have discovered in more than one thousand hours of study on this most controversial subject.

CHAPTER TWO

OBVIOUS OBSERVATIONS

"There exists no document from the ancient world witnessed by so excellent a set of textual and historical testimonies, and offering so superb an array of historical data on which the intelligent decision may be made. An honest (person) cannot dismiss a source of this kind. Skepticism regarding the historical credentials of Christianity is based upon an irrational bias."

Clark Pinnock
Professor of Interpretations
McMasters University
Toronto

In my attempt to refute Christianity, I made nine acute observations of the resurrection that I previously had been totally unaware of.

OBSERVATION #1—Testimony of History

Before my research on the resurrection, I had never realized there was so much positive historical, literary and legal testimony supporting its validity.

Roman history scholar

Professor Thomas Arnold, for 14 years the headmaster of Rugby, author of the three-volume *History of Rome,* and holder of the chair of modern history at Oxford, was well acquainted with the value of evidence in determining historical facts.

This great scholar said, "I have been used for many years to study the histories of other times, and to examine and weigh the evidence of those who have written about them, and I know of no one fact in the history of mankind which is proved by better and fuller evidence of every sort, to the understanding of a fair inquirer, than the great sign which God hath given us that Christ died and rose again from the dead."[1]

Textual critic

Brooke Foss Wescott, an English scholar, said, "Taking all the evidence together, it is not too much to say that there is no historic incident better or more variously supported than the resurrection of Christ. Nothing but the antecedent assumption that it must be false could have suggested the idea of deficiency in the proof of it."[2]

Professor of ancient history

Dr. Paul L. Maier, professor of ancient history at Western Michigan University, concluded that, "If all the evidence is weighed carefully and fairly, it is indeed justifiable, according to the canons of historical research, to conclude that the tomb in which Jesus was buried was actually empty on the morning of the first Easter. And no shred of evidence has yet been discovered in literary sources, epigraphy or archaeology that would disprove this statement.[3]

Chief justice

Lord Caldecote, Lord Chief Justice of England, has written: "My faith began with and was grounded on what I thought was revealed in the Bible. When, particularly, I came to the New Testament, the Gospels and other writings of the men who had been friends of Jesus Christ seemed to me to make an overwhelming case, merely as a matter of strict evidence, for the fact therein stated. . . . The same approach to the cardinal test of the claims of Jesus Christ, namely, His resurrection, has led me as often as I have tried to examine the evidence to believe it as a fact beyond dispute."[4]

Legal authority

One man who was highly skilled at dealing with evidence was Dr. Simon Greenleaf. He was the famous Royall Professor of Law at Harvard University and succeeded Justice Joseph Story as the Dane Professor of Law in the same university. The rise of Harvard Law School to its eminent position among the legal schools of the United States is to be ascribed to the efforts of these two men. Greenleaf produced his famous three-volume work, *A Treatise on the Law of Evidence*, which still is considered one of the greatest single authorities on this subject in the entire literature of legal procedure.

Greenleaf examined the value of the historical evidence for the resurrection of Jesus Christ to ascertain the truth. He applied the principles contained in his three-volume treatise on evidence. His findings were recorded in his book, *An Examination of the Testimony of the Four Evangelists by the Rules of Evidence Administered in the Courts of Justice*.

Greenleaf came to the conclusion that, according to the laws of legal evidence used in courts of law, there is more evidence for the historical fact of the resurrection of Jesus Christ than for just about any other event in history.

Attorney general

An Englishman, John Singleton Copley, better known as Lord Lyndhurst, is recognized as one of the greatest legal minds in British history. He was the solicitor-general of the British government, attorney-general of Great Britain, three times High Chancellor of England, and elected as High Steward of the University of Cambridge, thus holding in one lifetime the highest offices ever conferred upon a judge in Great Britain.

Upon Copley's death, among his personal papers were found his comments concerning the resurrection in the light of legal evidence and why he became a Christian: "I know pretty well what evidence is; and I tell you, such evidence as that for the resurrection has never broken down yet."[5]

Lord Chief Justice of England, Lord Darling, once said that "no intelligent jury in the world could fail to bring in a verdict that the resurrection story is true."[6]

Rationalistic lawyer

Dr. Frank Morrison, a lawyer who had been brought up in a rationalistic environment, had come to the opinion that the resurrection was nothing but a fairy-tale happy ending which spoiled the matchless story of Jesus. He felt that he owed it to himself and others to write a book that would present the truth about Jesus and dispel the mythical story of the resurrection.

Upon studying the facts, however, he, too, came to a different conclusion. The sheer weight of the evidence compelled him to conclude that Jesus actually did rise from the dead. Morrison wrote his book — but not the one he had planned. It is titled, *Who Moved the Stone?* The first chapter, very significantly, is, "The Book That Refused To Be Written."

Literary genius

The literary scholar, C.S. Lewis, former professor of Medieval and Renaissance literature at Cambridge University, when writing about his conversion to Christianity, indicated that he believed Christians "to be wrong."

The last thing Lewis wanted was to embrace Christianity. However, "Early in 1926 the hardest boiled of all the atheists I ever knew sat in my room on the other side of the fire and remarked that the evidence for the historicity of the Gospels was really surprisingly good. 'Rum thing,' he went on. 'All that stuff of Frazer's about the Dying God. Rum thing. It almost looks as if it had really happened once.'

"To understand the shattering impact of it, you would need to know the man (who has certainly never since shown any interest in Christianity). If he, the cynic of cynics, the toughest of the toughs, were not — as I would still have put it — 'safe,' were could I turn? Was there then no escape?"

After evaluating the basis and evidence for Christianity, Lewis concluded that in other religions there was "no such historical claim as in Christianity." His knowledge of literature forced him to treat the Gospel record as a trustworthy account. I was by now too experienced in literary criticism to regard the Gospels as myth.

Finally, contrary to his strong stand against Christianity, Professor Lewis had to make an intelligent decision:

"You must picture me alone in that room in Magdalen, night after night, feeling, whenever my mind lifted even for a second from my work, the steady, unrelenting approach of Him whom I so earnestly desired not to meet. That which I greatly feared had at last come upon me. In the Trinity Term of 1929 I gave in, and admitted that God was God, and knelt and prayed: perhaps, that night, the most dejected and reluctant convert in all England."[7]

One of my main reasons for writing *The Resurrection Factor* is to present the historical evidence that these men, and countless others like them, discovered when they were confronted with the statement that "on the third day the tomb was empty."

OBSERVATION #2—Resurrection Foretold

Christ actually predicted He would rise on the third day. His claims are substantiated throughout the four Gospels. When Jesus was going up to Jerusalem, He took the Twelve Disciples aside and said to them, "Behold, we are going up to Jerusalem. And the Son of man will be delivered to the death.

They will deliver Him to the Gentiles to mock, and to scourge, and to crucify Him. And on the third day He will be raised up."[8]

Mark points out in his Gospel that "He began to teach them that the Son of Man must suffer many things, and be rejected by the elders, and the chief priests, and the scribes, and be killed, and after three days rise again."[9]

John confirms this when he writes: "Jesus answered and said to them, 'Destroy this temple, and in three days I will raise it up.' The Jews therefore said, 'It took forty-six years to build this temple, and will you raise it up in three days?' But he was speaking of the temple of his body."[10]

OBSERVATION #3—Historical Basis

The historical fact of the resurrection is the very basis for the truth of Christianity. To put it simply, the resurrection of Jesus Christ and Christianity stand or fall together. One cannot be true without the other.

Risk all on resurrection

The Apostle Paul emphasized this point when he wrote, "But if there is no resurrection of the dead, not even Christ has been raised; and if Christ has not been raised, then our preaching is vain; your faith also is vain. Moreover we are even found to be false witnesses of God, because we witnessed against God that He raised Christ, whom He did not raise, if in fact the dead are not raised. For if the dead are not raised, not even Christ has been raised; and if Christ has not been raised, your faith is worthless."[11]

Dr. J.N.D. Anderson, professor of oriental law and the director of the Institute of Advanced Legal Studies at the University of London, concluded his research on the resurrection by saying, "It seems to me inescapable that anyone who chanced to read the pages of the New Testament for the first time would come away with one overwhelming impression, that there is a faith firmly rooted in certain allegedly historical events, a faith which would be false and misleading if those events had not actually taken place, but which — if they did take place — is unique in its relevance and exclusive in its demands on our allegiance."[12]

The New Testament goes one step further and teaches that the resurrection was the one thing that declared Jesus to be the Son of God.[13]

The resurrection was so crucial that Jesus was willing to risk all on its eventuality.

Even Dr. David Friedrick Strauss, an unbelieving skeptic who has severely criticized anything supernatural in the Gospels, was forced to acknowledge the fact that the resurrection is the "touchstone, not of the life of Jesus only, but of Christianity itself." It "touches Christianity to the quick" and is "decisive for the whole view of Christianity."

To say that Jesus placed a lot of emphasis on His resurrection is putting it mildly.

A Hindu bewildered

Everything that Jesus Christ taught, lived and died for depended upon His resurrection. Adherents of other religions are especially hard pressed to understand this emphasis. Almost all other religions are based upon a theological dictum or ideology, not upon the historical fact of its founder's identity or an event in time or space. The Christian faith's dependence upon history is almost incredulous to many Hindus.

Leslie Newbigin records the astonishment of a Ramakrishna Mission teacher. This devout and educated Hindu was bewildered by a Christian's claim that his Christian faith depended upon "the substantial historical truth of the record concerning Jesus in the New Testament."

The Hindu, not understanding Christianity, thought it "seemed axiomatic that such vital matters of religious truth could not be allowed to depend upon the accidents of history. If the truths which Jesus exemplified and taught are true, then they are true always and everywhere, whether a person called Jesus ever lived or not."[14]

OBSERVATION #4—Intelligent Faith

My fourth observation on Christianity was quite an eye-opener. It had crossed my mind many times that the followers of Christ seemed to exercise a blind, ignorant faith. H.L.

Mencken best expressed my former attitude about the Christian faith when he said, "Faith may be defined briefly as an illogical belief in the occurrence of the improbable."

The more I studied the historical-biblical Christian faith the more I realized it was an "intelligent faith." When an individual in the Scriptures was called upon to exercise faith, it was an intelligent faith. Jesus said, "You shall know the truth (not ignore it) and the truth shall make you free."[15]

A lawyer asked Jesus, "Which is the greatest commandment?" Jesus replied, "(to) love the Lord your God with all your heart . . . and with all your mind."[16] Never is an individual called upon to commit intellectual suicide in trusting Christ as Savior and Lord. Instead, a believer is instructed to be ready always to give an answer (an intelligent one) as to why he believes.[17]

Dr. George Eldon Ladd observes that, "Faith does not mean a leap in the dark, an irrational credulity, a believing against evidences and against reason. It means believing in the light of historical facts, consistent with evidences, on the basis of witnesses."

OBSERVATION #5—Possibility of Miracles

One must be careful in investigating the fact of the resurrection, so as not to rule it out historically because of one's bias against anything hinting of the supernatural or miraculous.

There is an attitude that surfaces repeatedly when exploring history. It is what I call the "Hume hangover." It is the argument by Hume that belief can be justified by probability and that probability is based upon the uniformity or consistency of nature. In other words, we are right in believing experiences that are normal to ordinary human experience. Anything that is unique so far as normal human experience is concerned — such as a miracle — should be rejected.

For example, which is more probable: The witnesses of Christ's resurrection were mistaken, or Jesus was raised from the dead?

According to Hume's "modern scientific attitude" the answer is obvious, because miracles simply can't happen.

A natural explanation

Another way of expressing this biased view of history is that we live in a closed universe in which no element of the supernatural can intervene. In other words, every event (past, present and future) must have a natural explanation. This rules out totally the intervention of the supernatural. No matter what happens or how strong the evidence, this attitude dictates that the supernatural or miraculous must be rejected, even in spite of the evidence.

A philosopher concludes

I was invited to be a guest lecturer in a philosophy class. The professor also was the department head. After I presented literary and historical evidence for the deity of Christ, the professor began to badger me with questions and accusations on the resurrection. After about ten minutes, a student interrupted and asked the professor a very perceptive question.

"Sir, what do you think happened that first Easter?"

The professor looked at me, then back at the student.

"I don't know what happened," he said, cautiously. Then before the student could comment, he added, "But it wasn't a resurrection!"

"Is your answer the result of examining the evidence?" the student responded.

The reply was, "No! It is because of my philosophical outlook."

At another major university, several students took my first book, *Evidence That Demands a Verdict*, to the chairman of the history department for evaluation. After several months, one of the students visited the chairman and asked for his opinion of it.

"It contains some of the most conclusive arguments historically for Christianity I've ever read," the professor responded.

The student got all excited. Then the department head added, "But I won't come to the same conclusion as Mr. McDowell."

"Why?" the student asked, puzzled.

"Because of my philosophical outlook," the answer came back.

There was no lack of evidence. The conclusion was reached in spite of it.

Limitations of Hume

Dr. Lawrence Burkholder, chairman of the Department of the Church at the Harvard Divinity School, admits that his approach to history had been greatly influenced by Hume's argument that for something to be true it must conform to the uniformity of nature. After realizing that every historical event is, to some extent, or in some way unique, he confessed, "I'm beginning to feel the limitations of Hume."[18]

Dr. Burkholder says that Hume's argument against miracles "is limiting the possibility of accepting what in later times and events I find to have been a fact. He is telling me I really can't believe anything unless it corresponds to past experience. But I find myself increasingly refusing to predict the future. I find myself becoming much more modest when it comes to saying what is possible and what is not possible, what may happen in the future and what may not happen. And this same modesty is beginning to take the form of a reluctance on my part to say what could have happened in the past and what could not have happened."[19]

Professor Burkholder adds, ". . . it seems to me I have some right at least to be open to the possibility that something may have happened which by analogy we call the resurrection."[20]

Professor Clark Pinnock, speaking of a confidence in Hume's methodology and the need to naturalize all historical events, points out that "the experience against miracles is uniform only if we know that all the reports about miracles are false, and this we do not know. No one has an infallible knowledge of 'natural laws,' so that he can exclude from the outset the very possibility of unique events. Science can tell us what *has* happened, but it cannot tell us what *may* or *may not* happen. It observes events; it does not create them. The historian does not dictate what history can contain; he is open to whatever the witnesses report. An appeal to Hume bespeaks ignorance of history."[21]

Dr. Wolfhart Pannenberg of the University of Munich adds, "The question . . . whether something happened or not at a given time some thousand years ago can be settled only by historical argument. . . ."[22]

Historical research needed

Dr. John Warwick Montgomery, writing about those who still adhere to a closed system (all events have to have a natural explanation), exclaims: "Since Einstein, no modern has had the right to rule out the possibility of events because of prior knowledge of 'natural law.' The only way we can know whether an event *can* occur is to see whether in fact it *has* occurred. The problem of miracles, then, must be solved in the realm of historical investigation, not in the realm of philosophical speculation."[23]

With the passing of the Newtonian epoch we need to leave room for the unpredictable, the unexpected and the incalculable element in the universe.[24]

Dr. Vincent Taylor, a prominent New Testament critic, warns against too great a dogmatism. Concerning the limitations of science in evaluating the miraculous he writes: "In the last 50 years we have been staggered too often by discoveries which at one time were pronounced impossible. We have lived to hear of the breaking up of the atom, and to find scientists themselves speaking of the universe as 'more like a great thought than like a great machine.' This change of view does not, of course, accredit the miraculous; but it does mean that, given the right conditions, miracles are not impossible; no scientific or philosophic dogma stands in the way."[25]

Frenchman Ernest Renan denounced the resurrection of Jesus Christ. He admitted to starting his research of Christ's life with the assumption, "There is no such thing as a miracle. Therefore the resurrection did not take place." An attitude like that never would be tolerated in a court of law. Renan's conclusion about Christ's resurrection was *not* based upon historical inquiry but rather upon philosophical speculation.

This mind set resembles that of the man who said, "I have made up my mind — don't confuse me with the facts."

OBSERVATION #6—Fact Not Fable

Another eye-opener to me was the observation that the followers of Christ knew the difference between "fact" and "fable," between "reality" and "fantasy." For years I'd heard the charge that, at the time of Jesus, people were prone to believe myths. Critic Rudolph Bultman would have us believe His contemporaries were naive and primitive. However, research reveals a tremendous exaggeration regarding the naivete of first-century man.

The apostle Peter exclaimed, "We did not follow cleverly devised tales when we made known to you the power and coming of our Lord Jesus Christ, but we were eye-witnesses . . ."[26] And the apostle Paul warned people not to "pay attention to myths and endless genealogies . . ."[27]

Even though, in the first century, men did not have as great a knowledge of the universe and the laws of nature as we do today, they knew that blind men usually stay blind. That's why they were astonished when Jesus healed the blind man.

"Since the beginning of time," they said, "it has never been heard that anyone opened the eyes of a person born blind."[28]

They also knew that *dead men tend to stay dead.* Paul's treatment on Mars Hill in Greece[29] shows that the resurrection was just as difficult for people to believe in the ancient world as it is today.

Then there was Thomas, dubbed "doubting Thomas." He must have been from "Hahvaad." He said "Look, not every day does somebody get raised from the dead. I need a little evidence." He emphasized that, "Unless I shall see in His hands the imprint of the nails, and put my finger into the place of the nails, and put my hand into His side, I will not believe."

At this point, Jesus said to Thomas, "Reach here your finger, and see My hands; and reach here your hand, and put it into my side; and be not unbelieving, but believing." Thomas answered, "My Lord and my God!"

OBSERVATION #7—Scientific Method Ineffective

Many people advocate that nothing can be accepted as true unless it can be proven scientifically. When speaking on historical aspects of the resurrection in a university classroom, I am constantly confronted with the question, "Can you prove it scientifically?"

I immediately reply, "No." The modern scientific method does not apply when researching the factuality of the events surrounding the death, burial and resurrection of Jesus Christ. Science is unable to investigate it.

Observation through repetition

Scientific proof is based on showing that something is a fact by repeating the event in the presence of the person questioning the fact. A controlled environment is set up. There observations are made, data drawn, and hypotheses empirically verified.

The "scientific method . . . is related to measurement of phenomena and experimentation or repeated observation."[30] Dr. James B. Conant, former president of Harvard, writes: "Science is an interconnected series of concepts and conceptual schemes that have developed as a result of experimentation and observations."[31]

The Basic Dictionary of Science describes scientific knowledge as that "knowledge based on the observation and testing of facts."[32] *The Harper Encyclopedia of Science* describes scientific method as ". . . techniques of controlled observation employed in the search for knowledge."[33]

Science is limited

The main thrust of science is being able to collect data from continuous observation of the testing of a hypothesis. Therefore the "modern scientific" method is applicable only to repeatable events or facts. As a unique event in history, the resurrection of Jesus Christ is outside the realm of scientific inquiry. The inability to repeat in a controlled environment invalidates the key technique of the scientific method. In *More Than a Carpenter,* I develop the difference between the scientific method and the legal method of determining truth.

OBSERVATION #8—Historical Criteria

The resurrection of Christ must be examined by the same criteria as is any other past event in history. The faith of the early church was founded on experiences in the factual realm. For example, the followers of Christ said He showed Himself alive to them by "many convincing proofs.[34] Luke used the work *tekmerion.* That connotes a "demonstrable proof."

It became apparent to me that my research would have to include the historical criteria for truth if I were to discover what really happened that first Easter.

Sufficient evidence needed

We live in a world that demands adequate evidence for belief. It is the responsibility of *The Resurrection Factor* to set forth that evidence for the resurrection.

Wolfhart Pannenberg is professor of systematic theology at the University of Munich, Germany. He has been concerned primarily with questions of the relationship between faith and history. This brilliant scholar says, "Whether the resurrection of Jesus took place or not is a historical question, and the historical question at this point is inescapable. And so the question has to be decided on the level of historical argument."[35]

The evidence must be approached with an honest, fair view of history. The investigation must not be prejudiced by preconceived notions or conclusions. There is a compelling need to let the evidence speak for itself.

Historian Ronald Sider writes about the need for objectivity in historical research: "What does the critical historian do when his evidence points very strongly to the reality of an event which contradicts his expectations and goes against the naturalistic view of reality? I submit that he must follow his critically analyzed sources. It is unscientific to begin with the philosophical presupposition that miracles cannot occur. Unless we avoid such one-sided presuppositions, historical interpretation becomes mere propaganda.

"We have a right to demand good evidence for an alleged event which we have not experienced, but we dare not judge reality by our limited experience. And I would suggest that we have good evidence for the resurrection of Jesus of Nazareth."[36]

Proper approach

The Erlangen historian Ethelbert Stauffer gives further suggestions on how to approach history: "What do we (as historians) do when we experience surprises which run counter to all our expectations, perhaps all our convictions and even our period's whole understanding of truth? We say as one great historian used to say in such instances: 'It is surely possible.' And why not? For the critical historian nothing is impossible."[37]

Historian Philip Schaff adds to the above: "The purpose of the historian is not to construct a history from preconceived notions and to adjust it to his own liking, but to reproduce it from the best evidences and to let it speak for itself."[38]

If one is to judge the historicity of Jesus, then he ought to be judged as impartially as any other figure in history. Dr. F.F. Bruce of the University of Manchester in England testifies that "the historicity of Christ is as axiomatic for an unbiased historian as the historicity of Julius Caesar. It is not historians who propagate the 'Christ-myth' theories."[39]

A critical attitude

The ultimate test historically concerning the resurrection is whether the purported facts are supported by the evidence.

At this point, one realizes that he must proceed with caution and carefully examine the data about Christ's resurrection. A critical historian would want to check out the witnesses; confirm the death by crucifixion; go over the burial procedures; confirm the reports of Jesus being alive on the third day and the tomb being empty. Then it would be sensible to consider every possible explanation of the above data. At this stage one would want to peruse other corroborative evidence and then draw an appropriate conclusion.

Sound interesting? This is what I will do in the following pages.

OBSERVATION #9—Reliable Historical Document

The New Testament provides the primary historical source for information on the resurrection. Because of this, many critics during the 19th and 20th centuries have attacked the reliability of these documents. The "ancient document" principle under the Federal Rules of Evidence permits the authentication of a document to be made by showing that the document (1) is in such condition as to create no suspicion concerning its authenticity; (2) was in a place where, if authentic, it would likely be, and (3) has been in existence 20 years or more at the time it is offered.[40]

Dr. John Warwick Montgomery, a lawyer, and dean of the Simon Greenleaf School of Law, comments about the application of the "ancient document" rule to the New Testament documents: "Applied to the gospel records, and reinforced by responsible lower (textual) criticism, this rule would establish competency in any court of law."[41]

F.C. Bauer, along with other critics, assumed that the New Testament Scriptures were not written until late in the second century A.D. He concluded that these writings came basically from myths or legends that had developed during the lengthy interval between the lifetime of Jesus and the time these accounts were set down in writing.

Dating of New Testament

By the end of the 19th century, however, archaeological discoveries had confirmed the accuracy of the New Testament manuscripts. Discoveries of early *papyri* manuscripts bridged the gap between the time of Christ and existing manuscripts from a later date. See my first book, *Evidence That Demands a Verdict,* for detailed information on the various manuscript discoveries.

These findings increased the confidence of scholars in the reliability of the Bible. William Albright, once the world's foremost biblical archaeologist, said: "We can already say emphatically that there is no longer any solid basis for dating any book of the New Testament after A.D. 80, two full generations before the date between 130 and 150 given by the more radical New Testament critics of today."[42]

Coinciding with the *papyri* discoveries, an abundance of other manuscripts came to light. Dr. John A.T. Robinson, lecturer at Trinity College, Cambridge, has been for years one of England's more distinguished critics. Robinson accepted the consensus typified by German criticism that the New Testament was written years after the time of Christ at the end of the first century. But, as "little more than a theological joke," he decided to investigate the arguments on the late dating of all the New Testament books, a field largely dormant since the turn of the century.

The results stunned him. He said that owing to scholarly "sloth," the "tyranny of unexamined assumptions" and "almost willful blindness" by previous authors, much of the past reasoning was untenable. He concluded that the New Testament is the work of the Apostles themselves or of contemporaries who worked with them and that all the New Testament books, including John, had to have been written before A.D. 64.

Robinson challenges his colleagues to try to prove him wrong. If scholars reopen the question, he is convinced, the results will force "the rewriting of many introductions to — and ultimately, theologies of — the New Testament."[43]

Manuscript authority

When I finished my research into biblical reliability and released *Evidence That Demands a Verdict* in 1973, I was able to document 14,000 manuscripts of the New Testament alone.

Last year I reissued and updated *Evidence* . . . because of the vast amount of new research material available. Now I am able to document 24,633 manuscripts of the New Testament alone.

The significance of the number of manuscripts documenting the New Testament is even greater when one realizes that in all of history the number two book in manuscript authority is *The Iliad*, by Homer. It has 643 surviving manuscripts.

The great number of manuscripts authenticating the New Testament motivated Sir Frederick Kenyon, one of the leading authorities on the reliability of ancient manuscripts, to write: "The interval, then, between the dates of original composition and the earliest extant evidence becomes so small as to be in fact negligible, and the last foundation for any doubt that the Scriptures have come down to us substantially as they were written now has been removed. Both the authenticity and the general integrity of the books of the New Testament may be regarded as finally established."[44]

F.F. Bruce makes the following observation: "The evidence for our New Testament writings is ever so much greater than the evidence for many writings of classical authors, the authenticity of which no one dreams of questioning."

He also states, "And if the New Testament were a collection of secular writings, their authenticity would generally be regarded as beyond all doubt."[45]

Some critics of the New Testament advocate that the early church created the "sayings" and "events" around the life of Jesus. Others assert that facts about the events surrounding the life of Jesus were written down so long after the fact that they were undoubtedly corrupted. Thus, it is alleged we do not have a trustworthy account of the actual words and life of Christ.

Short time period

What can be said to refute these allegations? There are many reasons for confidently believing that today we do have a reliable account of the actual words of Jesus and the events surrounding His life.

The first is that manuscript discoveries and subsequent historical research show that the time element between the events of Christ's life and the recording of them was not sufficient to affect their accuracy.

Dr. Paul L. Maier, professor of ancient history at Western Michigan University, writes: "Arguments that Christianity hatched its Easter myth over a lengthy period of time or that the sources were written many years after the event are simply not factual."[46]

Analyzing the critics' conclusions of late authorship, Albright wrote: "Only modern scholars who lack both historical method and perspective can spin such a web of speculation as that with which critics have surrounded the Gospel tradition."

He added that the period is "too slight to permit any appreciable corruption of the essential center and even of the specific wording of the sayings of Jesus."[47]

Concerning the manuscripts' trustworthiness Millar Burrows of Yale says: "Another result of comparing New Testament Greek with the language of the *papyri* is an increase of confidence in the accurate transmission of the text of the New Testament itself."[48]

He continues that "the texts have been transmitted with remarkable fidelity, so that there need be no doubt whatever regarding the teaching conveyed by them."[49] Howard Vos, researcher, declares that: "From the standpoint of literary evidence the only logical conclusion is that the case for the reliability of the New Testament is infinitely stronger than that for any other record of antiquity."[50]

Eyewitness accounts

A second reason for the trustworthiness of the New Testament records of Christ is that they were written by eyewitnesses or from eyewitness accounts.

Dr. Louis Gottschalk, historian, in writing about the examination of the accuracy of a source says, "Ability to tell the truth rests in part upon the witness's nearness to the event. *Nearness* is here used in both a geographical and a chronological sense."[51]

The writers of the New Testament recorded that they ". . . did not follow cleverly devised tales when we make known to you the power and coming of our Lord Jesus Christ, but we were eyewitnesses of His majesty."[52]

They said that Jesus "presented Himself [to them] alive, after His suffering, by many convincing proofs, appearing to them over a period of forty days."[53]

Luke, the physician, wrote: "Inasmuch as many have undertaken to compile an account of the things accomplished among us, just as those who from the beginning were eyewitnesses . . . it seemed fitting for me as well, having investigated everything carefully from the beginning, to write it out for you in consecutive order. . . ."[54]

Although eyewitnesses hold an honored place in a court of law, more and more the value of their firsthand testimony is being evaluated in the light of psychological factors influencing the individual: length of time, distance from subject, visibility, stress, fear, etc.[55]

Psychological factors

Dr. Elizabeth S. Loftus, professor of psychology at the University of Washington, writes that "people who witness fearful events remember the details of them less accurately than they recall ordinary happenings. Stress or fear disrupts perception and, therefore, memory. Stress can also affect a person's ability to recall something observed or learned during a period of relative tranquility."[56]

The eyewitness accounts of Jesus Christ after his resurrection are strengthened by Dr. Loftus' conclusions. The accounts were not fleeting glimpses of a stranger in a dark alley with a fear-producing weapon. His followers spent time with someone they knew and loved. Although there must have been stress and excitement (Jesus had to tell them not to be afraid) with the repetition of appearances (He appeared to them over a period of 40 days), they became more certain in their memories.

Obvious Observations

While the multiple number of New Testament eye-witnesses are not a 100% guarantee of reliability, it would be extremely difficult to argue that each one made the same mistake in identification. The eyewitness accounts of having seen Christ alive after His resurrection would be very convincing in a court of law, especially in view of the extensive testimony.

The hearsay rule

McCormick's *Handbook of the Law of Evidence*, an excellent treatise on analyzing evidence, observes that the legal system's insistence upon using only the most reliable sources of information is best manifested in the rule requiring that a witness who testifies to a fact which can be perceived by the senses must have had an opportunity to observe, and must have actually observed the fact.[57]

The emphasis of this *hearsay rule* is that "hearsay" is not admissible as evidence in a court of law. *The Federal Rules of Evidence* declares that a witness must testify concerning what he has firsthand knowledge of, not what had come to him indirectly from other sources.[58]

Concerning the value of one testifying "of his own knowledge," Dr. Montgomery points out that from a legal perspective the New Testament documents meet the demand for "primary-source" evidence. He writes that the New Testament record is "fully vindicated by the constant asseverations of their authors to be setting forth that 'which we have heard, which we have seen with our eyes, which we have looked upon, and our hands have handled.' "[59]

Firsthand knowledge

According to Matthew, the Gospel writer, the first persons to hear of the resurrection were Mary Magdalene "and the other Mary."[60] They were told of the event by an angel seated on the stone of the tomb. Any recounting of this by the two Marys would be hearsay, unless offered merely to prove that the angel had been there and spoken to them. If the two women reported in court the words of the angel in order to prove that Christ had risen, it would be hearsay, and prohibited. It is not the veracity of the angel that is doubted; rather, the hearsay rule questions the accuracy and perhaps honesty of the person recounting the tale.

This problem is solved, however, by Jesus' personal appearance to the women.[61] Because the women thus gained firsthand knowledge of the fact that Christ had been raised from the dead, they would be competent to testify in court. They had not witnessed the actual event, but their having seen the result sufficiently justified their conclusion that the resurrection had occurred.

Matthew also briefly reports Jesus' appearance to the 11 disciples.[62] Had an appearance not been made to the disciples personally, they could not have testified to Jesus' resurrection under the hearsay rule. Seeing Christ alive made the hearsay rule inapplicable.

Luke gives us the account of the two men of Emmaus to whom Christ appeared. These men demonstrated how quickly hearsay may be discounted. They did not believe the women's report of what the angels had told them. They believed that the tomb was empty; whether Christ was indeed alive was uncertain, for "Him they did not see."[63] It was not until Jesus revealed Himself to these two men that they were able to believe.

The book of Luke, like the books of Matthew and Mark, closes with Christ's appearance before all the disciples. Jesus clearly was aware of the normal suspicion of mere hearsay. The hearsay rule is evidence of this suspicion. We often are reluctant to believe what someone else has experienced; much less what someone else has been told.

The greatest example of this reluctance is Thomas, the doubter.[64] Despite the accounts of appearances to those men who probably were closer to Thomas than to any of the others, the story of Christ's resurrection still was incredible. He demanded firsthand knowledge before he would commit himself.

Written accounts

Are the written records of eyewitnesses reliable? *The Federal Rules of Evidence* says that recordings by witnesses are admissible where they can be shown "to have been made or adopted by the witness when the matter was fresh in his memory and to reflect that knowledge correctly."[65] Some might question whether Matthew and John recorded their recollections while still fresh in their memories. We don't know how soon after these great events the disciples wrote their Gospels. No matter how long, however, it can be convincingly argued that seeing alive again the same Person the two disciples had watched die three days earlier is simply not a forgettable event.

One can imagine the disciples saying years later, "I remember it as though it happened yesterday."

Presence of knowledgeable eyewitnesses

A third reason for historical reliability is that the New Testament accounts of the resurrection were circulated during the lifetimes of those alive at the time of the resurrection. Therefore, the accuracy of these accounts could have been confirmed or contradicted at that time.

When those who wrote the New Testament argued their case for the Gospel, they appealed to common knowledge concerning the facts of the resurrection.

Peter challenged his audience, "Men of Israel, listen to these words: Jesus the Nazarene, a man attested to you by God with miracles and wonders and signs which God performed through Him in your midst, just as you yourselves know."[66]

Presence of hostile eyewitnesses

Another reason there was no room for myths, legends, or inaccuracies in the accounts of the life and teachings of Christ is that they were circulated during the lifetime of knowledgeable people who were extremely hostile to the new Christian movement.

One primary means of evaluating the truthfulness of a witness is through the use of cross-examination, because cross-examination by an adverse party brings out the truthfulness of a witness and reveals the witness' possible bias or prejudice.[67]

Justice Ruffin in *State vs. Morris* amplifies the "cross-examination" principle: "All trials proceeded upon the idea that some confidence is due to human testimony, and that this confidence grows and becomes more steadfast in proportion as the witness has been subjected to a close and searching cross-examination."[68]

Concerning the value of the presence of "hostile witnesses" in applying the "cross-examination" principle to the proclamation of the resurrection, law professor Dr. John Montgomery writes, ". . . this rule underscores the reliability of testimony to Christ's resurrection which was presented contemporaneously in the synagogues — in the very teeth of opposition, among hostile cross-examiners who would certainly have destroyed the case for Christianity had the facts been otherwise."[69]

F.F. Bruce, the Rylands professor of biblical criticism and exegesis at the University of Manchester, says concerning the value of the New Testament records being scrutinized by vocal opponents: "Had there been any tendency to depart from the facts in any material respect, the possible presence of hostile witnesses in the audience would have served as a further corrective."[70]

There are three steps in historical testimony: observation, recollection and recording.[71] The "bitter enemies" of this new movement centering around Christ were ready to challenge any over-zealous follower who might have wanted to add a miracle or to sweeten up a story to make Christ more appealing. These "hostile witnesses" were ready to correct any distortion in the "observation, recollection and recording" of all that Jesus "did and taught."[72]

Stan Gundry, theologian, asks, "Is it possible that they would have allowed false statements to pass as facts concerning His life which they also knew so well? Christianity would have opened itself to ridicule if it had created such stories to perpetuate itself."[73]

The apostles, who surely desired to honor the Lord, would not have been a party to ascribing to Him facts that did not originate with Him. Further, hundreds of people in the early church must have been a powerful restraining factor in keeping the tradition true to fact.

Confirmation by archaeology

Louis Gottschalk writes that an author's or document's general credibility is dependent upon "the reputation of the author for veracity, the lack of self-contradiction within the document, the absence of contradiction by other sources, freedom from anachronisms, and the way the author's testimony fits into the otherwise known facts help to determine the general credibility."[74]

In other words, "Conformity or agreement with other known historical [geographic] or scientific facts is often the decisive test of evidence, whether of one or of more witnesses."[75]

Sir William Ramsay, one of the greatest geographers ever to have lived, was a student of the German historical school of the mid-19th century. He became firmly convinced that the book of Acts was a product of the mid-second century A.D. after making a topographical study of Asia Minor which compelled him to consider the writings of Luke. As a result of the overwhelming evidence uncovered in his research, he was forced to completely reverse his beliefs.

Luke's proven reliablity

Concerning Luke's ability as a historian, Ramsay concluded after 30 years of study that "Luke is a historian of the first rank; not merely are his statements of fact trustworthy . . . this author should be placed along with the very greatest of historians."[76]

Ramsay adds: "Luke's history is unsurpassed in respect of its trustworthiness."[77]

Luke at one time was considered incorrect for referring to the Philippian rules as *praetors*. According to the "scholars," two *duumuirs* would have ruled the town. However, as usual, Luke was right. Findings have shown that the title of *praetor* was employed by the magistrates of a Roman colony.

Luke's choice of the word *proconsul* as the title for Gallio[78] also has been proven correct, as evidenced by the Delphi inscription which states in part: "As Lucius Junius Gallio, my friend, and the proconsul of Achaia. . . ."

The Delphi inscription (A.D. 52) gives us a fixed time period for establishing Paul's ministry of one and one-half years in Corinth. We know this by the fact, from other sources, that Gallio took office on July 1, that his proconsulship lasted only one year, and that that same year overlapped Paul's work in Corinth.

Luke gives to Publius, the chief man in Malta, the title "leading man of the island."[79] Inscriptions have been unearthed which also give him the title, "first man."

Still another case for Luke's reliability is his usage of *politarchs* to denote the civil authorities of Thessalonica.[80] Since *politarch* is not found in classical literature, Luke again was assumed to be wrong. However, some 19 inscriptions now have been found that make use of the title. Interestingly enough, five of these refer to leaders in Thessalonica.

Archaeologists at first questioned Luke's implication that Lystra and Derbe were in Lycaonia and that Iconium was not.[81] They based their belief on the writings of Romans such as Cicero who indicated that Iconium was in Lycaonia. Thus, archaeologists said the book of Acts was unreliable. However, Sir William Ramsay found a monument that showed Iconium to be a Phrygian city. Later discoveries confirmed this.

Among other historical references made by Luke is that of "Lysanias the Tetrarch of Abilene"[82] at the beginning of John the Baptist's ministry in 27 A.D. The only Lysanias known to ancient historians was the one who was killed in 36 B.C. However, an inscription found near Damascus speaks of the "Freedman of Lysanias the Tetrarch" and is dated between 14 and 29 A.D.

It is no wonder that E.M. Blaiklock, professor of classics at Auckland University, concludes that "Luke is a consummate historian, to be ranked in his own right with the great writers of the Greeks."[83]

A true picture

F.F. Bruce, of the University of Manchester, notes: "Where Luke has been suspected of inaccuracy, and accuracy has been vindicated by some inscriptional evidence, it may be legitimate to say that archaeology has confirmed the New Testament record."[84]

Bruce comments on the historical accuracy of Luke: "A man whose accuracy can be demonstrated in matters where we are able to test it is likely to be accurate even where the means for testing him are not available. Accuracy is a habit of mind, and we know from happy (or unhappy) experience that some people are habitually accurate just as others can be depended upon to be inaccurate. Luke's record entitles him to be regarded as a writer of habitual accuracy."[85]

One can conclude that the New Testament gives an accurate portrait of Christ. This historical account of Him cannot be rationalized away by wishful thinking, historical manipulation or literary maneuvering.

Summary

In my attempt to refute Christianity, I made nine important observations:

1) The historical, literary and legal testimony supporting the resurrection of Jesus Christ is immense.

2) Jesus Christ Himself actually predicted that He would rise on the third day.

3) The resurrection of Jesus Christ is the sole fact that validates all the rest of Christianity.

4) The Christian faith is not a leap in the dark but a faith based on intelligent reasoning.

5) While it is not honest, many have ruled out the possibility of the resurrection because of their bias against miracles.

6) The followers of Christ were not ignorant. They knew the difference between fact and fable.

7) The scientific method cannot be used in investigating the resurrection because events in history cannot be repeated in the presence of the investigators.

8) The same criteria must be applied when examining the resurrection of Jesus Christ as is applied to any other event of history.

9) Scholarly evidence exists in abundance to document that the New Testament (the primary source on the resurrection) can survive the most severe scrutiny according to all rules for examining testimony and according to the findings of modern archaeology.

CHAPTER THREE

SECURITY PRECAUTIONS

*"No trial in the long and tragic annals of
mankind has had more momentous consequences
than that of an obscure Jewish religious leader
who came into Jerusalem with a small band
of followers and was arrested, convicted
and executed over nineteen hundred years ago.
To be sure, there have been other landmark
cases in history, like those of the Hebrew
prophet, Micah the Morashtite, and the
Greek philosopher, Socrates, the heresy hearing
of the Italian scientist, Galileo, and the
excommunication of the Dutch-Jewish
philosopher, Spinoza, as well as more recent
trials that are still the subject of controversy.
Yet none has had a greater impact, for good
and for ill, upon the lives of men, than
the trial and death of Jesus of Nazareth."*

Robert Gordis
*Jewish Theological Seminary
of America*

SECURITY PRECAUTION #1—The Trial

Jesus was brought for trial before the Roman governor, Pontius Pilate. All available evidence shows Pilate to have been an extremely cruel and merciless despot. Philo records that he was responsible "for countless atrocities and numerous executions without any previous trial."[86]

Archaeological confirmation of Pilate

Until 1961 the only historical references to Pontius Pilate were literary. Then two Italian archaeologists excavated the Mediterranean port city of Caesarea that served as the Roman capital of Palestine. During the dig they uncovered a two-by-three foot inscription in Latin. Antonio Frova was able to reconstruct the inscription. To his surprise it read: "Pontius Pilate, Prefect of Judea, has presented the Tiberium to the Caesareans." This was the first archaeological discovery of a historical reference to the existence of Pilate.

Six trials

One needs to realize that Jesus Christ went through six distinct trials. One was before Annas, the high priest;[87] another was before Caiaphas;[88] the third one was before the Sanhedrin;[89] the fourth one was before Pilate;[90] the fifth one before Herod;[91] and the sixth was back before Pilate.[92] There were three Jewish trials and three Roman trials.

Why all this concern over one man? Both the Roman and Jewish authorities had various reasons for being concerned about Christ's remaining free.

Political motive

First, there was the political motive. When Jesus replied to the governor's question,[93] "Are you the King of the Jews?" by saying, "It is as you say," He gave them grounds for execution.

Justice Haim Cohn, a learned member of the Supreme Court of Israel, in an article entitled "Reflections on the Trial of Jesus," says, "There can be no doubt that a confession such as this was sufficient in Roman law for conviction of the defendant."[94] The offense was punishable with death[95] and the governor was vested with the *jus gladi* (the right to pass the death sentence).[96]

Professor R.E. Grant, of the University of Chicago, in his paper "The Trial of Jesus in the Light of History" believed both Jews and Romans alike interpreted Christ's remark as a reference to kingship. Grant believes the idea of kingship that Jesus preached was interpreted by both the Jews and the Romans as carrying with it the seeds of rebellion against the Roman power.[97]

Solomon Zeitlin writes in the *Jewish Quarterly Review* that "the Roman authorities punished not only the individuals who incited the people against the Romans, but the leaders of the people as well. In some respects, we may say that the Jewish leaders were held as hostage for the obedience of the Jewish people to the Roman State. Many Jewish leaders, by circumstance of the political condition, had to act as informers against some of the dissenters and revolutionaries among their own brethren in order to save their own lives."[98]

Jesus was considered by the Jewish authorities to be a menace, not only to the Jewish economic situation but also to the political welfare of the Jewish State which was dominated by the Romans.[99] It was to the advantage of both the Jews and the Romans, therefore, that the high priest would inform the Roman authorities of Jesus' activities.

The Jewish problem

Dr. David Flusser of the Hebrew University in Jerusalem observes that the danger of a Jewish insurrectionist whose followers might break loose at any moment was a problem to both the Jewish as well as the Roman authorities. From the Jewish authorities' point of view, Dr. Flusser writes: "Failure to bring the potential menace to the governor's attention while it could be checked might well prove costly to them in the long run and lead to reprisals and to stricter oversight. Moreover, it would be a very smart move. Should there be an outbreak of protest from the self-styled prophet's supporters, far better that the object of the popular hatred be the Roman governor rather than they. Thus, regardless of whether the Jewish authorities could or could not logically themselves inflict the death penalty, it was but common sense to let Pilate take the step."[100]

The Roman problem

From the point of view of Pilate, Flusser writes, the matter was equally clear: "Should he refuse to follow the advice of the local leaders, who knew their tricky and incomprehensible fellow countrymen as no Roman could ever hope to do, and should this individual prove a serious menace, well might he tremble at the thought of his own fate at the hands of the outraged Tiberius."[101]

However, Flusser is the first to point out that Pilate's fear of incurring Jewish wrath was nothing compared to the Jews' fear of enduring the wrath of Rome.

Historian Paul Maier observes that there had been "a dozen uprisings in Palestine since Pompey first conquered the land in 63 B.C. — most of them subdued by Roman force — another Messianic rebellion under Jesus of Nazareth would only shatter the precarious balance of authority and, bleeding Rome's patience dry, might lead to direct occupation by Roman legions."[102]

For political reasons Jesus was a menace.

Economical motive

Another motive for wanting Jesus out of the way was economical. After He upset the tables of the moneychangers in the Temple, they feared He might further upset commercialization inside the Temple. Possibly they feared an uprising against Temple practices by the thousands of Passover pilgrims who were hailing Him as the Messiah.

Religious motives

Still other motives for wanting to deal with Jesus were personal and religious. This "religious fanatic" was acquiring quite a following and causing personal embarrassment to the Jewish leaders. Many of their teachings were being questioned by those influenced by Jesus.

Two Jewish trial courts

The Jewish legal system was made up of two different Sanhedrins. One Sanhedrin was composed of 23 members who tried cases involving capital punishment.[103] The other Sanhedrin of 71 could serve as a trial court for cases involving the head of State, the high priest, or for offenses against the State or the Temple. The Sanhedrin of 71 could not try a case involving capital punishment. It was probably the Sanhedrin of 23 that tried Jesus. One was located in every major city in Judea.[104]

Finally after three Jewish trials and three Roman trials, the Jewish authorities, in conjunction with the Roman authorities, delivered up Jesus to be crucified.[105]

Various "security precautions" were taken to make sure that when Jesus was dead He would remain dead and buried.

SECURITY PRECAUTION #2—Death by Crucifixion

Ancient literary texts and artifacts say very little about the early practice of death by crucifixion. But there are some inferences that it was practiced.

History of crucifixion

From various references in the works of Herodotus and Thucydides it can be ascertained that if the Persians did not invent the crucifixion, they at least practiced it on a large scale. One of the best sources concerning the practice of crucifixion is the Behistum Inscription in which Darius tells that he had crucified the various rebel leaders he conquered.

One possible reason for the rise in popularity of death by hanging on a cross is that the Persians had consecrated the ground to their god Ormayed. This type of execution would not defile the ground because the body did not touch it.

Alexander the Great introduced crucifixion into the

Mediterranean world — mainly Egypt and Carthage. From all indications, the Romans learned the practice from the Carthaginians.

A cruel death

Death by crucifixion developed into one of the world's most disgraceful and cruel methods of torture. Cicero called it "the most cruel and hideous of tortures."[106] Will Durant wrote that "even the Romans . . . pitied the victims."[107]

Flavius Josephus, the Jewish historian, who was an advisor to Titus during the siege of Jerusalem, had observed many crucifixions and called them "the most wretched deaths."[108] Josephus reports that when the Romans threatened to crucify one of the Jewish prisoners, the entire Machaerus garrison surrendered in order to obtain safe passage. Crucifixion was so gruesome and degrading that the Romans usually excluded Roman citizens and reserved it for slaves to discourage uprisings, or for those rebelling against the Roman government. It was mainly used in political cases.

The accusation against Christ emphasizes this use of crucifixion: "And they began to accuse Him, saying, We found this man misleading our nation, and forbidding to pay taxes to Caesar, and saying that He Himself is Christ, a King."[109]

His accusers were cognizant of the fact that ten years earlier Tiberius had declared that a judge could immediately execute one who had rebelled against Rome.

Crucifixion, for the most part, was unknown in Jewish criminal law. The Jews advocated execution by stoning, burning, beheading and strangling (Sanh. VII.I). Hanging later was permitted (Targum Ruth 1.17)[110] Where the Jewish criminal law prescribed "hanging on a gibbet," it was not as a death penalty, but rather as a degrading punishment after death for idolaters and blasphemers who already had been stoned to death.

The hanging, in compliance with the law,[111] identified the accused as having been accursed of God. Usually crucifixion, whether Roman or Jewish, indicated what type of crime an individual had been accused of.

The custom of whipping

After the verdict of crucifixion had been pronounced by the court, it was customary to tie the accused to a post at the tribunal. The criminal was stripped of his clothes, then severely whipped by the lictors or scourgers.

The whip, known as a flagrum, had a sturdy handle to which were attached long leather thongs of varying lengths. Sharp jagged pieces of bone and lead were woven into them. The Jews were limited by their law to 40 lashes. The Pharisees, with their emphasis on strict adherence to the law, would limit their lashes to 39, so that if they miscounted they would not break their law. The Romans had no such limitations. Out of disgust or anger, the Romans could totally ignore the Jewish limitation, and probably did so in the case of Jesus.

A medical perspective

Dr. C. Truman Davis, a medical doctor who has meticulously studied crucifixion from a medical perspective, describes the effects of the Roman flagrum used in whipping: "The heavy whip is brought down with full force again and again across [a person's] shoulders, back and legs. At first the heavy thongs cut through the skin only. Then, as the blows continue, they cut deeper into the subcutaneous tissues, producing first an oozing of blood from the capillaries and veins of the skin, and finally spurting arterial bleeding from vessels in the underlying muscles. The small balls of lead first produce large, deep bruises which are broken open by subsequent blows. Finally the skin of the back is hanging in long ribbons and the entire area is an unrecognizable mass of torn, bleeding tissue. When it is determined by the centurion in charge that the prisoner is near death, the beating is finally stopped."[112]

Eusebius, a third-century historian, confirms Dr. Davis'

description when he writes: "The sufferer's veins were laid bare, and the very muscles, sinews, and bowels of the victim were open to exposure."[113] Will Durant says it left the body "a mass of swollen and bloody flesh."[114] It was the custom after flagellation to mock the individual, and the Roman soldiers did this to Christ. They placed a purple robe, supposedly signifying royalty, around His shoulders and a "crown of thorns" on His head.

A crown of thorns

Which thorn or type of thorn was used is uncertain. One comes from a plant called the Syrian Christ Thorn, a shrub about 12 inches high with two large, sharp, recurved thorns at the bottom of each leaf. This plant is common in Palestine, especially around the site of Golgotha were Christ was crucified.

Another plant, simply called the Christ Thorn, is a dwarf-sized shrub anywhere from 4' to 8' high. Its thorns are easy to pick. The branches also can be bent easily to form a crown, and the thorns, in pairs of different lengths, are stiff — like nails or spikes.

After placing the crown of thorns on Christ's head, they began to mock Him saying, "Hail, the King of the Jews." They also spit on Him and beat Him with a rod. Then they led Him away to be crucified.

The crossbar burden

A man condemned to be crucified had to carry his own crossbar from prison to the place of his execution. This crossbar has a unique history. Dr. Pierre Barbet's research shows that "the *furca* was a piece of wood in the form of an inverted V on which the shaft of the two-wheeled carts was rested when they were in the stables. When a slave was to be punished, the *furca* was placed astride the nape of his neck, his hands were bound to the two arms, and he was marched through the neighborhood, while he was made to proclaim his offense."

Dr. Barbet points out that since "a *furca* was not always obtainable, they began to use a long piece of wood, which was used for barring doors and was called the *patibulum* (from *patere*, to be open)."[115] The *patibulum* weighed approximately 110 pounds and was strapped to the victim's shoulders.

Crucifixion with nails

Upon reaching the execution site, the condemned person was nailed or bound by ropes to the cross. Many have questioned the historical accuracy of the nailing of the hands and feet. The reason for this skepticism is that there has been almost zero evidence of it in history.

Dr. J.W. Hewitt, in his *Harvard Theological Review* article entitled, "The Use of Nails in the Crucifixion," said, "To sum up, there is astonishingly little evidence that the feet of a crucified person were ever pierced by nails."[116] He went on to say that the victim's hands and feet were bound by ropes to the cross.

For years Dr. Hewitt's statement was quoted as the final word. The conclusion, therefore, was that the New Testament account of Christ being nailed to the cross was false and misleading. Crucifixion by use of nails was considered legendary. It was believed that nails would have ripped the flesh and could not have supported a body on the cross.

A dead man speaks

Then, a revolutionary archaeological discovery was made in June 1968. Archaeologist V. Tzaferis, under the direction of the Israeli Department of Antiquities and Museums, discovered four cave-tombs at the site of Giv'at ha-Mivtar (Ras el-Masaref) just north of Jerusalem near Mount Scopus. These family tombs, hewn out of soft limestone, date from the late second century B.C. to 70 A.D. Composed of forecourts which led to burial chambers, they housed 15 limestone ossuaries that contained the bones of 35 individuals.

In many of the containers, moisture had helped preserve the bones. Evidence of death by violence was discovered in five cases: one by a blow from a mace, another by an arrow, and another by crucifixion.[117] The skeletal remains were examined by Dr. N. Haas of the department of anatomy of the Hebrew University and the Hadassah Medical School.

Tomb I — dated back to the first century A.D. by its pottery — contained a number of ossuaries. In Ossuary 4, inscribed with the name Yohanan Ben Ha'galgal, were found the bones of an adult male and of a child. A large 7-inch spike had been driven through the heel bone, and both legs had been fractured. Haas reported: "Both the heel bones were found transfixed by a large iron nail. The shins were found intentionally broken. Death caused by crucifixion."[118]

This discovery from the time of Christ adds solid archaeological evidence that the method of nailing individuals to a wooden cross as a means of execution, as mentioned in the New Testament, no longer is based solely upon literary evidence.

The bones in Ossuary #4 confirm another passage in the New Testament: "The soldiers therefore came, and broke the legs of the first man, and of the man who was crucified with Him; but coming to Jesus, when they saw that He was already dead, they did not break His legs."[119]

Haas concluded that Yohanan had both his leg bones broken by a *coup de grace*, and that "the percussion, passing the already crushed right calf bones, was a harsh and severing blow for the left one, attached as they were to the sharp-edged wooden cross."[120]

Purpose for breaking of legs

Here again is concrete evidence to support the New Testament passage on the breaking of the legs. To understand why the legs were broken, one must study the means of execution. The soldiers would feel for the depression at the front of the wrist, then drive the heavy wrought-iron spike through at that point. Next, the legs were placed together and large nail was driven through them. The knees were left moderately flexed, and a seat (known as a *sedecula*) was attached to the cross for the buttocks of the victim.

Haas observed of Yohanan that "the feet were joined almost parallel, both transfixed by the same nail at the heels, with the legs adjacent; the knees were doubled, the right one overlapping the left; the trunk was contorted; the upper limbs were stretched out, each stabbed by a nail in the forearm."[121]

The following diagram gives a visual picture of the body's position when nailed to the cross.

Then the usual method of terminating a crucifixion was known as crucifracture. It consisted of the breaking of the leg bones to prevent the victim from pushing upward in order to breathe and avoid final suffocation.

Dr. Truman Davis, the M.D. whom I quoted before, describes what happens to the human body after a short time of exposure on the cross: "As the arms fatigue, great waves of cramps sweep over the muscles, knotting them in deep, relentless, throbbing pain. With these cramps comes the inability to push Himself upward. Hanging by His arms, the pectoral muscles are paralyzed and the intercostal muscles are unable to act. Air can be drawn into the lungs, but cannot be exhaled. Jesus fights to raise Himself in order to get even

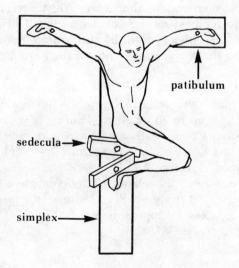

patibulum

sedecula

simplex

one short breath. Finally, carbon dioxide builds up in the lungs and in the bloodstream and the cramps partially subside. Spasmodically, He is able to push Himself upward to exhale and bring in the life-giving oxygen."[122]

After a while, orthostatic collapse through insufficient blood circulating to the brain and heart would follow. The only way the victim could avoid this was to push up by his feet so the blood could be returned to some degree of circulation in the upper part of his body.

When the authorities wanted to hasten death or terminate the torture, the victim's legs were broken below the knees with a club. This prevented him from pushing himself upward to relieve the tension on the pectoral or chest muscles. Either rapid suffocation or coronary insufficiency followed. In the case of Christ, the legs of the two thieves crucified with Him were broken, but Christ's were not because the executioners observed He already was dead.

Spilling of blood and water

One of the executioners thrust a spear into Christ's side and, as recorded in John 19:34, ". . . immediately there came out blood and water."

Davis relates that there was "an escape of watery fluid from the sac surrounding the heart. We, therefore, have rather conclusive post-mortem evidence that [Christ] died, not the usual crucifixion death by suffocation, but of heart failure due to shock and constriction of the heart by fluid in the pericardium."[123]

Dr. Stuart Bergsma, a physician and surgeon, writes about the "blood and water," saying: "A small amount of pericardial fluid, up to 20 or 30 cc's, normally is present in good health. It is possible that with a wound piercing the pericardium and heart, enough pericardial fluid might escape to be described as water."[124]

Dr. Bergsma further relates that post-mortem findings in several cases of ruptured hearts show "the pericardial cavity was occupied by approximately 500 cc's of fluid and freshly clotted blood."[125]

Two other medical authorities state that, in instances of a ruptured heart, "death is usually so sudden that in many cases the person is seen merely to fall over dead or is found dead. The great majority of cases were complete ruptures of the wall of the heart, producing large hemopericardia."[126]

Roman customs applied

After the victim was nailed to the cross, a description of his crime was fastened to the top part of the cross. The sign (or *titulus*) in Christ's case read, "Jesus the Nazarene, the King of the Jews."

Following their custom,[127] Roman soldiers usually divided up the victim's garments. However, in the case of Christ, there was only one piece. Therefore, they cast lots for it.

Pilate required certification of Christ's death before the body could be turned over to Joseph of Arimathea.[128] He consented to Christ's being removed from the cross only after four executioners had certified His death.

A job well done

The efficiency of execution by crucifixion was quite well-known in the time of Christ. Dr. Paul L. Maier, professor of ancient history at Western Michigan University, writes, "True, there is a recorded instance of a victim being taken down from a cross and surviving. The Jewish historian Josephus, who had gone over to the Roman side in the rebellion of 66 A.D., discovered three of his friends being crucified. He asked the Roman general Titus to reprieve them, and they were immediately removed from their crosses.

"Still, two of the three died anyway, even though they apparently had been crucified only a short time. In Jesus' case, however, there were the additional complications of scourging and exhaustion, to say nothing of the great spear thrust that pierced His rib cage and probably ruptured His pericardium. Romans were grimly efficient about crucifixions: Victims did *not* escape with their lives."[129]

SECURITY PRECAUTION #3—Solid Rock Tomb

The body of Christ was placed in a new tomb, hewn out of a solid rock, in a private burial area. Jewish tombs usually had an entrance 4-1/2-to-5-feet high. After the resurrection, the women panicked at seeing the tomb disturbed and ran back and told the men. Peter and John ran to the tomb, and the Bible says John "leaned over and looked in." John leaned over because the entrance was only 4-1/2-to-5 feet high. He wasn't a midget, and he didn't want a headache.

Most tombs of this period had a forecourt that led into the burial chamber. A rectangular pit in the center of the burial chamber enabled one to stand upright.[130] Around the chamber were a number of *loculi* or couches upon which the body was placed. Often, a raised section served as a pillow.[131]

Early sepulchers had a groove, or trough, cut into the rock in front of them to hold the stone which sealed them. The trough was designed in such a way that its lowest part lay immediately in front of the entrance. When the block holding back the stone was removed, the stone would roll down and lodge itself in front of the opening.

SECURITY PRECAUTION #4—Jewish Burial

A fourth "security precaution" was the method of burial. The New Testament is very clear that the burial of Christ followed the customs of the Jews.

Never overnight

He was taken down from the cross and covered with a sheet. The Jews were very strict about not allowing the body to remain all night upon the cross: "If he is left (hanging) overnight, a negative command is thereby transgressed. For it is written, his body shall not remain all night upon the tree, but thou shalt surely bury him the same day for he is hanged (because of) a curse against God — as if to say why was he hanged? — Because he cursed the name (of God); and so the name of heaven [God] is profaned."[132]

The body was immediately transported to the place of burial — in Christ's situation, to a private tomb near Golgotha where He was crucified.

Body preparation

In preparing a body for burial, the Jews would place it on a stone table in the burial chamber. The body first would be washed with warm water. *The Babylonian Talmud* (the commentaries of the Jews) record that the washing of the body was so important to proper burial, the Jews permitted it even on the Sabbath.[133]

A.P. Bender, in a *Jewish Quarterly Review* article entitled, "Beliefs, Rites, and Customs of the Jews, Connected with Death, Burial, and Mourning," writes that according to the ancient customs of the Jews: "The water required for the cleansing of the dead has to be warmed. The ceremonial of washing the corpse must not be performed by one person alone, not even in the case of a child. The dead must likewise not be moved from one position to another by fewer than two persons. The corpse is laid on a board, with its feet turned towards the door, and covered with a clean sheet. . . . The corpse is now washed from head to foot in lukewarm water, during which process the mouth is covered, so that no water should trickle down it.

"First, the dead lies with face lifted upward; it is next inclined upon the right side while the left side and part of the back are being washed, and is then turned on to the left side while the right side and the remaining portion of the back are being subjected to the same treatment, the corpse being afterwards laid on its back. In some cases the nails are cut, but generally they are simply cleaned with a special kind of pin, while the hair is often arranged in the manner in which it was worn in life. . . .

"While this ceremonial is being carried out, some verses are recited by those who officiate, concluding with the words, 'And I will sprinkle clean water upon you, and you shall be clean.' (Ezekiel xxxvi. 25).

"The board on which the corpse lay is cleansed, and all the water that may have been spilt around about is cleared up, so that no one should pass over it. The overturning of the board is fraught with danger, and any one might die in consequence within three days afterwards (Testament of R. Jehuda Chasid. VI.)."[134]

Use of aromatic spices

It was the custom, as verified in the New Testament, to prepare the corpse (after cleansing) with various types of aromatic spices.

In the case of Christ's burial, 100 pounds of spices were used. One might regard this as substantial, but it was no great amount for a leader. For example, Gamaliel, grandson of the distinguished Jewish scholar Hillel, also was a contemporary of Jesus. Saul of Tarsus studied under him. When Gamaliel died, they used 86 pounds of spices. Josephus, the Jewish historian, records that when Herod died, it required 500 servants to carry the spices.[135] So 100 pounds was not unusual.

Strips of linen cloth

After all the members of the body were straightened, the corpse was clothed in grave vestments made out of white linen. There could not be the slightest ornamentation or stain on the cloth.[136] The grave linens were sewn together by women. No knots were permitted. For some this was to indicate that the mind of the dead was "disentangled of the cares of this life"[137] — to others, it indicated the continuity of the soul through eternity. No individual could be buried in fewer than three separate garments.

The author is very skeptical of the Shroud of Turin. The cloth is believed by many to be the very burial cloth of Christ. My extensive reservations are covered in detail in my recent book (with Don Stewart), *Answers to Tough Questions*.

At this point, the aromatic spices, composed of fragments of a fragrant wood pounded into a dust known as aloes, were mixed with a gummy substance known as myrrh. Starting at the feet, they would wrap the body with the linen cloth. Between the folds were placed the spices mixed with the gummy substance. They would wrap to the armpits, put the arms down, then wrap to the neck. A separate piece was wrapped around the head. I would estimate an encasement weighing between 117 and 120 pounds.

John Chrysostom, in the fourth century A.D., commented that "the myrrh used was a drug which adheres so closely to the body that the graveclothes could not easily be removed."[138]

SECURITY PRECAUTION #5—Very Large Stone

Matthew records in his writings that a large stone was rolled against the front of the tomb.[139] Mark said the stone was extremely large.[140] In today's language, he would have said, "Wow! Get a loada' that rock!"

Just how large was that "Wow, get a loada' that rock" stone?

Twenty men could not move it

In the Mark 16:4 portion of the Bezae manuscripts in the Cambridge Library in England, a parenthetical statement was found that adds, "And when He was laid there, he (Joseph) put against the tomb a stone which *20 men could not roll away.*"

The significance of this is realized when one considers the rules for transcribing manuscripts. It was the custom that if a copier was emphasizing his own interpretation, he would write his thought in the margin and not include it within the text. One might conclude, therefore, that the insert in the text was copied from a text even closer to the time of Christ, perhaps, a first-century manuscript. the phrase, then, could have been recorded by an eyewitness who was impressed with the enormity of the stone which was rolled against Jesus' sepulcher.

One-and-a-half to two tons

After my lecture at Georgia Tech, two engineering professors went on a tour of Israel with other Georgia Tech faculty members. They remembered the comments I had made about the large size of the stone. So, being engineers, they took the type of stone used in the time of Christ and calculated the size needed to roll against a 4-1/2-to-5-foot doorway.

Later, they wrote me a letter containing all the technical terms, but on the back put their conclusions in simple language.

They said a stone of that size would have to have had a minimum weight of 1-1/2-to-2 tons. No wonder Matthew and Mark said the stone was extremely large.

One might ask, "If the stone were that big, how did Joseph move it into position in the first place?" He simply gave it a push and let gravity do the rest. It had been held in place with a wedge as it sat in a groove or trench that sloped down to the front of the tomb. When the wedge was removed, the heavy circular rock just rolled into position.

SECURITY PRECAUTION #6—Roman Security Guard

Jewish officials panicked, because thousands were turning to Christ. To avoid a political problem, it was to the advantage of both the Romans and the Jews to make sure Jesus was put away for good.

So the chief priests and Pharisees gathered together and said to Pilate, "Sir, we remember that when He was still alive that deceiver said, 'After three days I am to rise again.' Therefore, give orders for the grave to be made secure until the third day, lest the disciples come and steal Him away and say to the people, 'He has risen from the dead,' and the last deception will be worse than the first."[141]

Pilate said to them, "You have a guard; go, make it as secure as you know how." And so "they went and made the grave secure, and along with the guard they set a seal on the stone."

Some people would argue that Pilate said, "Look, you have your Temple police. You take your Temple police, go make it secure."

The Temple police

Now, if you want to say it's a Temple guard, you need to realize who made up that guard. It consisted of a group of 10 Levites who were placed on duty at different places at the Temple. The total number of men on duty was 270. This represented 27 units of 10 each. The military discipline of the Temple guard was quite good. In fact, at night, if the captain approached a guard member who was asleep, he was beaten and burned with his own clothes. A member of the guard also was forbidden to sit down or to lean against something when he was on duty.

A Roman guard

However, I am convinced it was the Roman guard that was placed at the grave of Christ to secure it.

A.T. Robertson, noted Greek scholar, says that this phrase is in the present imperative and can refer only to a Roman guard, and not the Temple police. According to him, Pilate literally said, "Have a guard."

Robertson adds that the Latin form *koustodia* occurs as far back as the Oxyrhynchus papyrus in reference to the Roman guard. The Jews knew Pilate wanted to keep the peace, so they were sure he'd give them what they wanted.

What was the Roman guard?

A Roman "custodian" did a lot more than care for a building. The word "custodian" represented the guard unit of the Roman Legion. This unit was probably one of the greatest offensive and defensive fighting machines ever conceived.

One helpful source for understanding the importance of the Roman guard is Flavius Vegitius Renatus. His friends called him Vegitius. A military historian, he lived several hundred years after the time of Christ when the Roman army started to deteriorate in its discipline. He wrote a manual to the Roman Emperor Valentinian to encourage him to instill the methods of offensive and defensive warfare used by the Romans during the time of Christ. Called *The Military Institutes of the Romans*, it is a classic today.

Vegitius wanted to see the Roman armies restored to the efficiency and might which characterized them at the time of Christ. These armies were great because they were highly disciplined. He wrote, "Victory in war does not depend entirely upon numbers of mere courage; only skill and discipline will insure it. We find that the Romans owed . . . the conquest of the world to no other cause than continual military training, exact observance of discipline in their camps and unwearied cultivation of the other arts of war."

There are two other excellent sources. At Indiana University, Dr. George Currie did his doctoral dissertation on the Roman custodian, and Dr. Smith edited a dictionary entitled, *Dictionary of Greek and Roman Antiquities*.

The force of the Roman guard

These and other sources point out that the Roman guard was not a one-, two-, or three-man force. Supercilious pictures of the tomb of Jesus Christ show one or two men standing around with wooden spears and mini-skirts. That's really laughable.

A Roman guard unit was a 4-to-16-man security force. Each man was trained to protect six feet of ground. The 16 men in a square of four on each side were supposed to be able to protect 36 yards against an entire battalion and hold it.

Normally what they did was this: four men were placed immediately in front of what they were to protect. The other 12 were asleep in a semi-circle in front of them with their heads pointing in. To steal what these guards were protecting, thieves would first have to walk over those who were asleep. Every four hours, another unit of four was awakened, and those who had been awake went to sleep.

They would rotate this way around the clock.

Historian Dr. Paul Maier writes, "Peter would be guarded by four squads of four men each when imprisoned by Herod Agrippa (Acts 12), so sixteen would be a minimum number expected *outside* a prison. Guards in ancient times always slept in shifts, so it would have been virtually impossible for a raising party to have stepped over all their sleeping faces" without waking them.[142]

High priest offers bribe

Even Matthew records that it was a multi-man force when he wrote that "*some* of the guard came into the city and reported to the chief priests all that had happened."[143]

A critic at this point might say, "See, they came to the high priest. It shows they were the Temple guard." The context is clear, however, that they came to the high priest because he had influence with the Roman authority and because it was the only possible way to save their necks. The high priest tried to bribe them (which would have been a mockery if they had been Temple police). He gave them money and told them what to tell the people. When the news reached Pilate, he said he (the high priest) would keep them from being killed. Normally, they would receive the death penalty, because the story was to be that they had fallen asleep while guarding the tomb.

It is significant that the governor had to be satisfied, because I have not been able to find any account in history — secular, Jewish or Christian — indicating that the Roman governor had anything at all to do with the Temple police.

Even if the guard at the tomb had been made up of Temple police, the security would have been no less thorough.

A fighting machine

T.G. Tucker, in his book, *Life in the Roman World of Nero and St. Paul*, describes one of these guards: "Over his breast, and with flaps over the shoulders, he will wear a corset of leather covered with hoop-like layers, or maybe scales, of iron or bronze. On his head will be a plain pot-like helmet or skull-cap of iron.

"In his right hand he will carry the famous Roman pike. This is a stout weapon, over 6 feet in length, consisting of a sharp iron head fixed in a wooden shaft, and the soldier may either charge with it as with a bayonet, or he may hurl it like a javelin and then fight at close quarters with his sword.

"On the left arm is a shield, which may be of various shapes. The shield is not only carried by means of a handle, but may be supported by a belt over the right shoulder. In order to be out of the way of the shield, the sword — a thrusting rather than a slashing weapon, approaching 3 feet in length — is hung at the right side by a belt passing over the left shoulder. . . . On the left side, the soldier wears a dagger at his girdle."[144]

Polybius, the Greek historian of the second century B.C., records that, in addition to all this, "the men are adorned with a crown made of feathers and with three upright feathers, either purple or black, about a foot and a half high; when they add these on the head along with the other arms, the man appears twice as big as he really is, and his appearance is striking and terrifying to the enemy. The men of the lowest property-classes also wear a bronze plate, 8 inches square, which they place in front of their chests and call the heart guard; this completes their armament. But those worth more than 10,000 drachmae, instead of wearing the heart guard, along with the rest of their equipment, wear a coat of mail."[145]

A severe discipline

Tucker points out that when a guard joined his unit "he is made to take a solemn oath that he will loyally obey all orders of his commander-in-chief, the emperor, as represented by that emperor's subordinates, his immediate officers. That oath he will repeat on each 1st of January and on the anniversary of the emperor's accession."[146]

SECURITY PRECAUTION #7—Roman Seal

Matthew records that "along with the guard they set a seal on the stone."[147] A.T. Robertson says this could be placed on the stone only in the presence of the Roman guards who were left in charge. Vegitius indicates the same thing. The purpose of this procedure was to prevent anyone from tampering with the grave's contents.

After the guard inspected the tomb and rolled the stone in place, a cord was stretched across the rock. This was fastened at either end with sealing clay. Finally, the clay packs were stamped with the official signet of the Roman governor.

A parallel to this is seen in Daniel: "And a stone was brought and laid over the mouth of the den; and the king sealed it with his own signet ring and with the signet rings of his nobles, so that nothing might be changed in regard to Daniel."[148]

Purpose of the seal

Henry Sumner Maine, member of the Supreme Council of India, formerly regius professor of the civil law at the University of Cambridge, speaking on the legal authority attached to the Roman seal, said, "Seals in antiquity were actually considered as a mode of authentication."

To authenticate something simply means to prove that it is real or genuine. So this seal on Jesus' tomb was a public testimony that Jesus' body was actually there. In addition, because the seal was Roman, it verified the fact that His body was protected from vandals by nothing less than the power and authority of the Roman Empire.

Anyone trying to move the stone from the tomb's entrance would have broken the seal and thus incurred the wrath of Roman law and power.

Grave robbers warned

In Nazareth, a marble slab was discovered with a very interesting inscription — a warning to grave robbers. It was written in Greek and says, "Ordinance of Caesar. It is my pleasure that graves and tombs remain perpetually undisturbed for those who have made them for the cult of their ancestors or children or members of their house. If, however, anyone charges that another has either demolished them, or has in any other way extracted the buried, or has maliciously transferred them to other places in order to wrong them, or has displaced the sealing or other stones, against such a one I order that a trial be instituted, as in respect of the gods, so in regard to the cult of mortals. For it shall be much more obligatory to honor the buried. Let it be absolutely forbidden for anyone to disturb them. In case of violation I desire that the offender be sentenced to capital punishment on charge of violation of sepulcher."[149]

Maier observes, "All previous Roman edicts concerning grave violation set only a large fine, and one wonders what presumed serious infraction could have led the Roman government to stiffen the penalty precisely in Palestine and to erect a notice regarding it specifically in Nazareth or vicinity."[150] It well could be a response to the commotion caused by Christ's resurrection.

Summary

Numerous religious fears and political motives caused both the Jews and the Roman governor, Pontius Pilate, to kill Jesus Christ. To make sure He remained dead and buried, six important security precautions were taken:
1) Christ was put to death by crucifixion, one of the most effective, cruel and hideous methods of execution ever devised.
2) The body of Christ was buried in a solid rock tomb.
3) Christ's body was wrapped with more than 100 pounds of spices according to precise Jewish burial customs.
4) The stone rolled in front of the tomb entrance weighed about two tons.
5) A Roman security guard, one of the most effective fighting units devised, was positioned to guard the tomb.
6) The tomb was sealed shut with the official authority and signate of Rome.

CHAPTER FOUR

FACTS TO BE RECKONED WITH

"If all the evidence is weighed carefully and fairly, it is indeed justifiable, according to the canons of historical research, to conclude that the tomb in which Jesus was buried was actually empty on the morning of the first Easter. And no shred of evidence has yet been discovered in literary sources, epigraphy, or archaeology that would disprove this statement."

Paul Maier
Historian

"I believe in the Resurrection, partly because a series of facts are unaccountable without it."

A.M. Ramsey
Archbishop of Canterbury

The Resurrection Factor

Now, something happened. Something happened almost 2,000 years ago that changed the course of history from B.C. (Before Christ) to A.D. (the Latin *Anno Domini* — the year of our Lord).

That "something" was so dramatic it completely changed 11 men's lives, so that all but one died a martyr's death.

That something was an empty tomb! An empty tomb that a 15-minute walk from the center of Jerusalem would have confirmed or disproved.

Even after 2,000 more years of history, mankind hasn't forgotten that empty tomb and the resurrection appearances of Jesus Christ.

If you wish to rationalize away the events surrounding Christ and His resurrection, you must deal with certain imponderables. In fact, you might say that both the Jews and the Romans outwitted themselves when they took so many precautions to make sure Jesus was dead and remained in the grave. These "security precautions" — taken with the trial, crucifixion, burial, entombment, sealing and the guarding of Christ's tomb — make it very difficult for critics to defend their position that Christ did not rise from the dead!

Consider these facts:

FACT #1—Broken Roman Seal

The first obvious fact was the breaking of the seal that stood for the power and authority of the Roman Empire. The consequences of breaking the seal were severe. The FBI and CIA of the Roman Empire were called into action to find the man or men responsible. When they were apprehended, it meant automatic execution by crucifixion upside down. Your guts ran into your throat. So people feared the breaking of the seal. Even the disciples displayed signs of cowardice, and hid themselves. And Peter went out and denied Christ three times.

FACT #2—The Empty Tomb

Another obvious fact after the resurrection was the empty tomb. The disciples of Christ did not go off to Athens or Rome to preach Christ raised from the dead; they went right back to the city of Jerusalem where, if what they were teaching was false, their message would have been disproved. The resurrection could not have been maintained for a moment in Jerusalem if the tomb had not been empty.

Dr. Paul Maier says, "Where did Christianity first begin? To this the answer must be: 'Only one spot on earth — the city of Jerusalem.' But this is the very *last* place it could have started if Jesus' tomb had remained occupied, since anyone producing a dead Jesus would have driven a wooden stake through the heart of an incipient Christianity inflamed by His supposed resurrection.

"What happened in Jerusalem seven weeks after the first Easter could have taken place only if Jesus' body were somehow missing from Joseph's tomb, for otherwise the Temple establishment, in its embroglio with the Apostles, would simply have aborted the movement by making a brief trip over to the sepulcher of Joseph of Arimathea and unveiling Exhibit A. They did not do this, because they knew the tomb was empty. Their official explanation for it — that the disciples had stolen the body — was an admission that the sepulcher was indeed vacant."[151]

Historical confirmation

There are both Jewish and Roman sources and traditions that acknowledge an empty tomb. These sources range from the Jewish historian Josephus to a compilation of fifth-century Jewish writings called the *Toledoth Jeshu*. Maier calls this "positive evidence from a hostile source, which is the strongest kind of historical evidence. In essence, this means that if a source admits a fact decidedly *not* in its favor, then that fact is genuine."[152]

The first counter-argument to the claim of an empty tomb was that the disciples stole the body.[153]

Gamaliel, who was a member of the Sanhedrin, put forth the suggestion that the Christian movement was of God;[154] he could not have done this if the tomb had been occupied, or if the Sanhedrin had known the whereabouts of Christ's body.

Even Justin Martyr in his *Dialogue with Trypho* relates that the Jerusalem authorities sent special representatives throughout the Mediterranean world to counteract the story of the empty tomb with the explanation that His followers stole the body. Why would the Jewish authorities bribe the Roman guard and propagate the "stolen body" explanation *if* the tomb was occupied?

Historian Ron Sider concluded that: "If the Christians and their Jewish opponents both agreed that the tomb was empty, we have little choice but to accept the empty tomb as a historical fact."[155]

Tom Anderson, former president of the California Trial Lawyers Association and co-author of the Basic Advocacy Manual of the Association of Trial Lawyers of America, says, "Let's assume that Christ did not rise from the dead. Let's assume that the written accounts of His appearances to hundreds of people are false. I want to pose a question. With an event so well publicized, don't you think that it's reasonable that one historian, one eyewitness, one antagonist would record for all time that he had seen Christ's body: 'Listen, I saw that tomb — it was not empty! Look, I was there, Christ did not rise from the dead. As a matter of fact, I saw Christ's body.' The silence of history is deafening when it comes to testimony against the resurrection."[156]

Strong evidence

Paul Maier observes: "Accordingly, if all the evidence is weighed carefully and fairly, it is indeed justifiable, according to the canons of historical research, to conclude that the sepulcher of Joseph of Arimathea, in which Jesus was buried, was actually empty on the morning of the first Easter. And no thread of evidence has yet been discovered in literary sources, epigraphy, or archaeology that would disprove this statement."[157]

The empty tomb is a silent testimony to the resurrection of Jesus Christ, that has never been refuted to this day.

FACT #3—Large Stone Moved

On that Sunday morning, the first thing that impressed the people who approached the tomb was the unusual

Facts To Be Reckoned With

position of that 1-1/2-to-2-ton stone that had been lodged in front of the doorway. All the Gospel writers mentioned the removal of the large stone.

Up an incline

For example, in Matthew 27, it is said that a "large stone was *rolled* against the entrance of the tomb." Here the Greek word used for roll is *kulio*, meaning "to roll." Mark used the same root word *kulio*. However, in Mark 16, he added a preposition to explain the position of the stone after the resurrection.

In Greek, as in English, to change the direction of a verb or to intensify it, you add a preposition. He added the preposition *ana*, which means "up or upward." So, *anakulio* can mean "to roll something up a slope or an incline." For Mark, then, to have used that verb, there would have had to be a slope or an incline coming down to the front of that tomb.

Away from

In fact, that stone was so far "up a slope" that Luke used the same root word *kulio*, but added a different preposition, *apo*. *Apo* can mean, according to the Greek lexicons, "a separation from," in the sense of "a distance from." *Apokulio*, then, means to roll one object from another object in a sense of "separation" or "distance from it."

Now, they saw the stone moved away in a sense of distance *from* "what"?

Let's go back to Mark 16. On Sunday morning, the women were coming to the tomb.

You might say, "Wait a minute! Why were these women coming to the tomb Sunday morning?" One reason was to anoint the body over the grave clothes with a mixture of spices and perfume.

Another might ask, "Why would they come since the Roman security unit was there guarding the grave?"

That's quite simple. The women did not know that the guard did not examine the body and secure the sepulcher until Saturday afternoon. On Friday they had watched the body prepared in a private burial area. They lived in the suburb of Bethany and therefore were not aware of the Roman and Jewish actions about putting extra security at the place of Christ's burial.

Let's go back to Mark 16 again.

The women were saying, "Who will roll away the stone for us from the entrance of the tomb?" Here, they used the Greek word for "entrance." That's logical, isn't it? *But*, when they got there they said, "Who rolled the stone away from . . . ?" and here they changed the Greek word for "the entrance" to the word used for the entire massive sepulcher. *Apokulio*, then, means "away from" in the sense of "distance from the entire massive sepulcher."

Picked up and carried

In fact, the stone was in such a position up a slope away from the entire massive sepulcher that John (chapter 20) had to use a different Greek verb, *airo*, which (according to the Arndt and Gingrish Lexicon) means "to pick something up and carry it away."

Now, I ask you, if the disciples had wanted to come in, tiptoe around the sleeping guards, then roll the stone over and steal the body, why would they have moved a 1-1/2-to-2-ton stone up a slope away from the entire massive sepulcher to such a position that it looked like someone had picked it up and carried it away? Those soldiers would have to have been deaf not to have heard that stone being moved.

FACT #4—Roman Guard Goes AWOL

The Roman guard fled. They left their place of responsibility. This has to be explained away because the military discipline of the Romans was exceptionally good. Justin, in his *Digest* #49, mentions all offenses which required the penalty of death: a scout remaining with the enemy (–3.4), desertion (–3.11; –5.1–3), losing or disposing of one's arms (–3.13), disobedience in war time (–3.15), going over the wall or rampart (–3.17), starting a mutiny (–3.19), refusing to protect an officer or deserting one's post (–3.22), a drafted man hiding from service (–4.2), murder (–4.5), laying hands on a superior or insult to a general (–6.1), leading flight when the example would influence others (–6.3), betraying plans to the enemy (–6.4; –7), wounding a fellow soldier with a sword (–6.6), disabling self or attempting suicide without reasonable excuse (–6.7), leaving the night watch (–10.1), breaking the centurion's staff or striking him when being punished (–13.4), escaping guard house (–13.5), and disturbing the peace (–16.1).

To the above, one can add "falling asleep." If it was not apparent which soldier had failed in duty, then lots were drawn to see who would be punished with death for the guard unit's failure.

Burned alive

One way a guard was put to death was by being stripped of his clothes, then burned alive in a fire started with the garments. The entire unit certainly would not have fallen asleep with that threat hanging over their heads. The history of Roman discipline and security testifies to the fact that if the tomb had not been empty the soldiers never would have left their position, nor would they have gone to the high priest. The fear of the wrath of their superiors and the possibility of the death penalty meant they paid close attention to the most minute details of their job.

Dr. George Currie, who studied carefully the military discipline of the Romans, wrote that fear of punishment "produced flawless attention to duty, especially in the night watches."[158]

Fear of punishment

Dr. Bill White is in charge of the Garden Tomb in Jerusalem. His responsibilities have caused him to study quite extensively the resurrection and subsequent events following the first Easter. White makes several critical observations about the Jewish authorities bribing the Roman guard:

"If the stone were simply rolled to one side of the tomb,

as would be necessary to enter it, then they might be justified in accusing the men of sleeping at their posts, and in punishing them severely. If the men protested that the earthquake broke the seal and that the stone rolled back under the vibration, they would still be liable to punishment for behaviour which might be labeled cowardice.

"But these possibilities do not meet the case. There was some undeniable evidence which made it impossible for the chief priests to bring any charge against the guard. The Jewish authorities must have visited the scene, examined the stone, and recognized its position as making it humanly impossible for their men to have permitted its removal. No twist of human ingenuity could provide an adequate answer or a scapegoat and so they were forced to bribe the guard and seek to hush things up."[159]

FACT #5—Graveclothes Tell A Tale

In a literal sense, against all statements to the contrary, the tomb was not empty because of an amazing phenomenon. After visiting the grave and seeing the stone rolled away, the women ran back and told the disciples. Then Peter and John took off running. John outran Peter, and upon arriving at the tomb he did not enter. Instead, he leaned over and looked in and saw something so startling that he immediately believed.

He looked over to the place where the body of Jesus had lain. There were graveclothes, in the form of the body, slightly caved in and empty — like the empty chrysalis of a caterpillar's cocoon. That was enough to make a believer out of anybody! He never did get over it!

The first thing that stuck in the minds of the disciples was not the empty tomb, but rather the empty graveclothes — undisturbed in their form and position.

FACT #6—His Appearances Confirmed

On several occasions, Christ appeared alive after the cataclysmic events of that first Easter.

Facts To Be Reckoned With

A principle to remember

When studying an event in history, it is important to investigate whether enough people who were participants or eyewitnesses to the event were alive when the facts about the event were published. This is helpful to validate the accuracy of the published report. If the number is substantial, the event can be fairly well established. For instance, if we all witness a murder, and in a week the police report turns out to be composed of fabricated lies, we as eyewitnesses can refute it.

In other words, when a book is written about an event, the accuracy of its content can be validated if enough people are alive at the time it is published who have been either eyewitnesses of, or participants in, the events recorded.

Several very important factors often are overlooked when investigating Christ's post-resurrection appearances to individuals. The first is the large number of witnesses of Christ after that first Sunday morning.

Fifty hours of eyewitnesses

One of the earliest records of Christ's appearing after the resurrection is by Paul.[160] The apostle appeals to his audience's knowledge of the fact that Christ had been seen by more than 500 people at one time. Paul reminds them that the majority of these people were still alive and could be questioned.

Dr. Edwin M. Yamauchi, associate professor of history at Miami University in Oxford, Ohio, emphasizes: "What gives a special authority to the list [of witnesses] as historical evidence is the reference to most of the 500 brethren being still alive. St. Paul says in effect, 'If you do not believe me, you can ask them.' Such a statement in an admittedly genuine letter written within 30 years of the event is almost as strong evidence as one could hope to get for something that happened nearly 2,000 years ago."[161]

Let's take the more than 500 witnesses who saw Jesus alive after His death and burial and place them in a courtroom. Do you realize that if each of these 500 people were to testify only six minutes each, including cross-examination, you would have an amazing 50 hours of firsthand eyewitness testimony? Add to this the testimony of many other eyewitnesses and you could well have the largest and most lopsided trial in history.

Variety of people

The second factor often overlooked is the variety of locations and people involved in Jesus' appearances.

Professor Merrill C. Tenney of Wheaton College writes that: "It is noteworthy that these appearances are not stereotyped. No two of them are exactly alike. The appearance to Mary Magdalene occurred in early morning; that to the travelers to Emmaus in the afternoon; and to the apostles in the evening, probably after dark. He appeared to Mary in the open air. Mary was alone when she saw Him; the disciples were together in a group; and Paul records that on one occasion He appeared to more than 500 at one time.[162]

"The reactions also were varied. Mary was overwhelmed with emotion; the disciples were frightened; Thomas was obstinately incredulous when told of the Lord's resurrection, but worshipped Him when He manifested Himself. Each occasion had its own peculiar atmosphere and characteristics, and revealed some different quality of the risen Lord."[163]

In no way can one say His appearances were stereotyped. (For details and chronology of the appearances, see Appendix: "Harmonious Account of the Post-resurrection Appearances.")

Hostile viewers

A third factor very crucial to interpreting Christ's appearances is that He also appeared to those who were hostile or unconvinced.

Over and over again I have read or heard people comment that Jesus was seen alive after His death and burial only by His friends and followers. Using this argument, they attempt to water down the overwhelming impact of the eyewitness accounts. But this line of reasoning is so pathetic it hardly deserves comment.

No author or informed individual would regard Saul of Tarsus to have been a follower of Christ. The facts show the exact opposite. He despised Christ and persecuted Christ's followers.[164] For Paul it was a life-shattering experience when Christ appeared to him.[165] Although Paul was not at the time a disciple, he later became one of the greatest witnesses for the truth of the resurrection.

Consider James, the brother of Jesus. The Gospel record indicates that His brothers were anything but believers.[166] Yet James later became a follower of his brother and joined the band of persecuted Christians.

Why? What caused such a change in his attitude? The historical explanation is that Jesus appeared also to James.[167]

The argument that Christ's appearances were only to His followers is an argument, for the most part, from silence. And arguments from silence can be dangerous. It is equally possible that all to whom He appeared became followers. This perhaps explains the conversion of many of the Jerusalem priests.[168]

No one acquainted with the facts can accurately say that Jesus appeared to just "an insignificant few."

FACT #7—Women Saw Him First

Another authenticating feature of the resurrection narrative is that the first appearances of the risen Christ were not to His disciples, but rather to women — to Mary Magdalene and the other women. This must have been an embarrassment to the apostles, Christ's inner circle. They were likely quite jealous.

According to Jewish principles of legal evidence, however, women were invalid witnesses. They did not have a right to give testimony in a court of law.

Unreliable testimony

Dr. Maier accurately observes that since the testimony of a woman was deemed unreliable, the "initial reaction of

the Eleven was understandably one of suspicion and dis-
belief. Again, if the resurrection accounts had been manufactured . . . women would *never* have been included in the
story, at least, not as first witnesses."[169]

Summary

The dramatic fact of the resurrection changed the course
of history. Two thousand years later man is still not the
same. Critics who wish to deny the resurrection of Jesus
Christ must adequately explain away seven historical
facts:

1) The feared power of Rome was ignored by the breaking of the Roman seal at the tomb.

2) Both the Jews and the Romans admitted that the tomb
was empty.

3) A two-ton stone was somehow moved from the tomb
entrance while a Roman guard stood watch.

4) A highly disciplined Roman military guard fled their
watch and had to be bribed by the authorities to lie about
what actually happened.

5) The undisturbed grave clothes no longer contained a
body.

6) Christ subsequently appeared to as many as 500 witnesses at one time in a variety of situations.

7) Because of the low Jewish view of the reliability of
women, manufacturers of a resurrection story would
never have selected them to be the first witnesses to the
fact.

CHAPTER FIVE

SEVERAL
ATTEMPTED
EXPLANATIONS

*"The purpose of the historian is not to construct
a history from preconceived notions and to
adjust it to his own liking, but to reproduce it
from the best evidence and to let it speak for itself."*
Philip Schaff
Historian

*"One must approach the evidence as honestly
and fairly as possible. We must not prejudice
our investigation by preconceived notions
or conclusions."*
Josh McDowell
Author

Two principles to consider

Many theories have been advanced, attempting to show that the resurrection of Jesus Christ was a fraud. I believe that many of the people who came up with these theories must have had two brains — one lost, and the other one out looking for it. Historians have to become anti-historical to invent some of their ideas.

Consider all the facts

When evaluating the options regarding what happened that first Easter, one needs to be conscious of two principles. First, the theories or alternate explanations must take into account all the facts surrounding the resurrection of Christ. Concerning various alternate theories in light of the evidence, J.N.D. Anderson, head of the Institute for Advanced Legal Studies in the University of London, emphasizes that "a point which needs stressing is that the evidence must be considered as a whole. It is comparatively easy to find an alternative explanation for one or another of the different strands which make up this testimony.

"But such explanations are valueless unless they fit the other strands in the testimony as well. A number of different theories, each of which might conceivably be applicable to part of the evidence but which do not themselves cohere into an intelligible pattern, can provide no alternative to the one interpretation which fits the whole."[170]

No preconceived conclusions

The second key principle to follow in the historical examination of events in history is not to force the evidence into a preconceived conclusion, but to let the evidence speak for itself. Historian Philip Schaff warns that "the purpose of the historian is not to construct a history from preconceived notions and to adjust it to his own liking, but to reproduce it from the best evidence and to let the evidence speak for itself."[171]

With these two principles in mind, let's examine the various theories which have been set forth as explanations for the events surrounding Christ's resurrection.

There are two basic alternatives. What happened concerning Christ's death, burial and resurrection has either a natural or supernatural explanation. After three days, Christ's tomb was either occupied or empty.

There are five natural-explanation theories. Each argues that Christ's tomb was still occupied and undisturbed after three days.

UNKNOWN TOMB THEORY

One of the earliest theories presented to explain everything away is that the tomb was unknown.

In Arlington National Cemetery near Washington, D.C., we have the Tomb of the Unknown Soldier. Here, it's the case of the unknown grave.

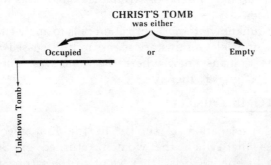

Who's got the body?

Professor Guignebert makes the following utterly unfounded statement: "The truth is that we do not know, and in all probability the disciples knew no better, where the body of Jesus had been thrown after it had been removed from the cross, probably by the executioners. It is more likely to have been cast into the pit for the executed than laid in a new tomb."[172]

One possible reason for this theory is that for years it was believed that those who were crucified were tossed into a common pit. The discovery in June 1968 of the remains of Yohanan Ben Ha'galgal in a family tomb outside of Jerusalem struck at the very heart of this theory, because Yohanan had been crucified. Yet he had been entombed at his burial.

Theory weaknesses

This theory also disregards totally the straightforward historical narrative about the events surrounding Christ's burial and the post-resurrection scene. The Gospel record indicates that Joseph of Arimathea took the body to his own private tomb. (Notice: It was not to a mass public burial grounds.) The body of Christ was prepared according to the burial customs of the Jews; the women sat opposite the tomb and watched.

If, for some unfathomable reason, the disciples and the women did not know the location of the tomb where Christ was laid, certainly Joseph of Arimathea did. It was his own private tomb.

The "unknown tomb" fabrication fails to apply either of the two principles of historical research discussed above. Also, the Romans knew where the tomb was. They had stationed a "guard" there.

WRONG TOMB THEORY

This explanation is similar to the first theory. It advocates that when the women returned on Sunday morning to honor Christ, they went to the wrong tomb.

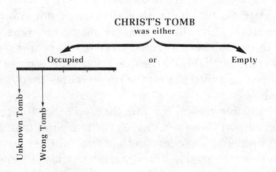

Several Attempted Explanations

Which tomb was it?

Professor Lake, one of the initiators of this theory, says: "It is seriously a matter for doubt whether the women were really in a position to be quite certain that the tomb which they visited was that in which they had seen Joseph of Arimathea bury the Lord's body. The neighborhood of Jerusalem is full of rock tombs, and it would not be easy to distinguish one from another without careful note. . . . It is very doubtful if they were close to the tomb at the moment of burial. . . . It is likely that they were watching from a distance, and that Joseph of Arimathea was a representative of the Jews rather than of the disciples. If so, they would have had but a limited power to distinguish between one rock tomb and another close to it. The possibility, therefore, that they came to the wrong tomb is to be reckoned with and it is important because it supplies the natural explanation of the fact that whereas they had seen the tomb closed, they found it open. . . .

"If it were not the same, the circumstances all seem to fall into line. The women came in the early morning to a tomb which they thought was the one in which they had seen the Lord buried. They expected to find a closed tomb, but they found an open one; and a young man . . . [who] guesses their errand, tried to tell them that they had made a mistake in the place. 'He is not here,' said he, 'see the place where they laid him,' and probably pointed to the next tomb. But the women were frightened at the detection of their errand, and fled. . . ."[173]

Fails the test

Professor Lake's theory does not meet the requirements of our two research principles. For one thing, it ignores just about all the evidence. Also, the theory constructs the evidence totally according to a preconceived notion.

For example, they have the young man at the tomb saying to the women, "He is not here, but see the place where they laid him." The complete text reads: "He is not here, for He has risen, just as He said. Come, see the place where He was lying."[174] Without any literary or historical justification whatsoever, the proponents of the "wrong tomb" theory preclude the phrase of the angel, "He is not here, for He has risen. . . ."

The literary evidence for including this phrase is as strong as any phrase of the New Testament. Although the wrong tomb theory sounds ingenious, it hinges on arbitrarily omitting the phrase, "He is risen." These women had carefully noted where the body of Jesus was interred less than 72 hours before (Matthew 27:61; Mark 15:47; Luke 23:55). This wasn't a public cemetery, but rather a private burial ground. Do you think that you or I, or these women, or any other rational person, would forget so quickly the place where a dearly beloved one was laid to rest?

Whole world went to the wrong tomb

To believe the "wrong tomb" theory, one would have to say that not only the women went to the wrong tomb, but that Peter and John ran to the wrong tomb; that the Jews then went to the wrong tomb, followed by the Jewish Sanhedrin and the Romans. You would then have to say that the guard returned to the wrong tomb and that Joseph of Arimathea, the owner of the tomb, also went to the wrong grave. And finally, you would have to say that the angel appeared at the wrong tomb. It would take a lot of faith (and blind faith at that) to believe something so absurd.

LEGEND THEORY

Some argue that the resurrection accounts are legends, cropping up years after the time of Christ.

In reality, this would be impossible. Resurrection accounts were circulated and written down by the original eyewitnesses. Paul related that in A.D. 56, there were almost 500 firsthand eyewitnesses who were still alive.

If it were possible to date the Gospels 200 or 300 years after the event of resurrection, the theory might be plausible. But in view of the facts, it is like a bucket without a bottom.

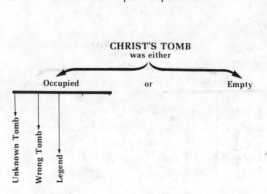

Many have tried to date the New Testament documents more than 100 years after Christ, and have miserably failed. Paul L. Maier, professor of ancient history at Western Michigan University, writes: "Arguments that Christianity hatched its Easter myth over a lengthy period of time or that the sources were written many years after the event are simply not factual."[175]

In analyzing much of New Testament criticism, William Albright wrote: "Only modern scholars who lack both historical method and perspective can spin such a web of speculation as that with which some critics have surrounded the Gospel tradition." Albright's own conclusion was that "a period of 20 to 50 years is too slight to permit any appreciable corruption of the essential content and even of the specific wording of the sayings of Jesus."[176] Dr. J.N.D. Anderson concludes that it is "almost meaningless to talk about legends when you're dealing with the eyewitnesses themselves."[177]

SPIRITUAL RESURRECTION THEORY

A fourth "occupied tomb" theory is that Christ's body decayed in the grave and that His real resurrection was spiritual.

A spiritual resurrection without the physical body would not be a resurrection at all, in the view of Palestinian Judaism. Dr. J.W. Drane observes that in Pharisaic Judaism it

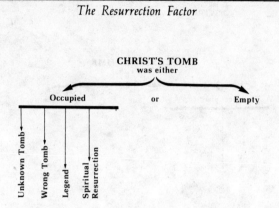

is "fairly certain that the general resurrection expectation in the Palestinian context envisaged the restoration of a body essentially identical with that which had been placed in the grave."[178] Drane points out that "a more spiritual resurrection was often envisaged, sometimes associated with the Greek idea. . . ."[179]

Jesus Himself completely demolished the "spiritual resurrection" theory. When His disciples, startled by seeing Him, thought they were seeing a spirit, Jesus admonished them, "See My hands and My feet, that it is I Myself; touch Me and see, for a spirit does not have flesh and bones as you see that I have."[180] Later, Christ ate fish with His followers, further demonstrating His flesh and bone. Matthew records that when they met Jesus they took hold of His feet and worshipped Him.[181] You don't grab the legs of a spirit!

This explanation completely ignores our two principles of research. The facts of the case don't even begin to fit the theory, and they are forced into a preconceived conclusion about what happened.

This theory also ignores the testimony of the Roman guard and of the Jewish high priest who bribed the soldiers and concocted the story that the disciples stole the body. It also ultimately disregards the empty tomb, graveclothes, etc.

HALLUCINATION THEORY

By far the most prevalent "occupied tomb" theory for explaining away the resurrection of Christ is that the people

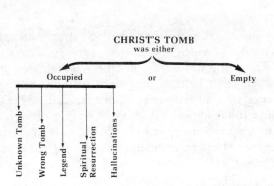

only thought they had seen Christ. In reality, they were hallucinating. In this way, all the post-resurrection appearances can be dismissed.

Definition of hallucinations

Could this hallucination theory coincide with the facts surrounding the many appearances of Christ to different individuals?

The word "hallucination" is an Anglicized form of the Latin term *alucination*, which means "a wandering of the mind, idle talk, prating."[182] The word "hallucination" didn't become a technical term in psychology and medicine until the 19th century.[183] Doctors Sarbin and Juhaz pointed out that "hallucination" is "perhaps unique among psychiatric terms in having remained essentially unaltered from the late 19th century to the present."[184]

The American Psychiatric Association's official glossary defines a "hallucination" as "a false sensory perception in the absence of an actual external stimulus."[185] The *Psychiatric Dictionary* defines it as "an apparent perception of an external object when no such object is present."[186] In an article by Dr. J.P. Brady of the Department of Psychiatrics at the University of Pennsylvania, School of Medicine, entitled "The Veridicality of Hypnotic Visual Hallucinations," he defines them as "the perception of objects or patterns of light which are not objectively present."[187]

These various definitions, plus psychological and medical observations, all agree that a hallucination is an apparent act of vision for which there is no corresponding external object. The optic nerve has not been stimulated by any outward waves of light or vibrations of the ether, but has been excited by a pure inner psychological cause.[188] Doctors Sarbin and Juhaz agree that "from the point of view of the person making the judgment, the hallucinator is imagining but claiming to be perceiving; he is responding to stimuli that are not there."[189]

Only certain people

Why is the hallucination theory so weak?

First, it contradicts various conditions which most psychiatrists and psychologists agree must be present to have a hallucination. Unless the appearances of Christ correspond to these essential conditions, referring to them as hallucinations is meaningless.

The first principle is that, generally, only particular kinds of people have hallucinations — usually only paranoid or schizophrenic individuals, with schizophrenics being the most susceptible.

In the New Testament, however, we have all different kinds of people, from different backgrounds, in different moods, and from different studies. (See page 85 for a description of the wide spectrum of psychological situations of the alleged "hallucinators.")

Very personal

Second, hallucinations are linked to an individual's subconscious and to his particular past experiences, making it very unlikely that more than two persons could have the same hallucination at the same time. Christ appeared to many people, and descriptions of the appearances involve great detail, like those which psychologists regard as determined by reality.

Christ also ate with those to whom He appeared.[190] And He not only exhibited His wounds,[191] but He also encouraged a closer inspection. An illusion does not sit down and have dinner with you, and cannot be scrutinized by various individuals at will.

A "hallucination" is a very private event — a purely subjective experience void of any external reference or object. If two people cannot initiate or sustain the same vision without any external object or reference, how could more than 500 do so at one time? It is not only contrary to this principle of hallucinations but also strongly militates against it. The many claimed hallucinations would be a far greater miracle than the miracle of the resurrection. This is what makes the view of Christ's appearances being hallucinations so ludicrous.

A false response

Another principle is that an illusion is an erroneous perception or a false response to sense stimulation. This runs contrary to all the appearances we have recorded for us regarding those who saw Christ.[192]

No favorable circumstances

Another principle of hallucinations is that they usually are restricted as to when and where they can happen. In the New Testament situations, favorable circumstances are missing. And the appearances recorded are much more than simple glimpses. Time was involved. You have 15 different appearances — at one time to over 500 people.

Consider the great variety of times and places: One was an early morning appearance to the women at the tomb. Another was the road to Emmaus, followed by a couple of private interviews in broad daylight. Another was by the lake early one morning. Indeed, the variety of times and places of Christ's appearances defies the hypothesis that they were mere visions.

No expectancy

A fifth principle is that hallucinations require of people an anticipating spirit or hopeful expectancy which causes their wishes to become father of their thoughts and hallucinations. As we look at the disciples, the last thing they expected was a resurrection. They thought Christ had been crucified, buried. . . . That was the end of it.

The late theologian, Paul Little, made an acute observation about the anticipatory attitude of the alleged "hallucinators": "Mary came to the tomb on the first Easter Sunday morning with spices in her hands. Why? To anoint the dead body of the Lord she loved. She was obviously not expecting to find Him risen from the dead. In fact, when the Lord finally appeared to the disciples, they were frightened and thought they were seeing a ghost."[193]

Not time enough

Hallucinations usually occur over a long period of time with noticeable regularity. What is interesting in applying this principle to the New Testament situation is that the appearances came to an abrupt end. They all stopped at the same time except for Christ's appearance to the apostle Paul whose circumstances and conditions were totally different.

Doesn't match the facts

A final principle is that hallucinations have no spectrum of reality — no objective reality whatsoever. The hallucination theory in no way accounts for the empty tomb, the broken seal, the guard units, and especially the subsequent actions of the high priests.

I am convinced of the shallowness of the critics' hallucination explanation. The above five theories (unknown tomb, wrong tomb, legend, spiritual resurrection only, and hallucinations) are naturalistic attempts to explain away the resurrection without the tomb itself being disturbed.

Summary

Two important principles must be followed in explaining what happened at the tomb of Jesus Christ on the first Easter:

1) The explanation must take into account all the known facts surrounding the resurrection events.

2) The evidence must not be forced into conforming to some preconceived conclusion. Over the course of history, five natural theories based on the premise that the tomb remained occupied have been advanced to explain away the resurrection:

A) The *Unknown Tomb Theory* argues that the executioners probably cast the body into an unknown burial pit.

B) The *Wrong Tomb Theory* says that the disciples mistook another tomb, which was empty, to be Christ's tomb.

C) The *Legend Theory* argues that accounts of Christ's resurrection did not crop up until years later.

D) The *Spiritual Resurrection Theory* argues that Christ's resurrection was only "spiritual" — His body decayed in the grave.

E) The *Hallucination Theory* suggests that all Christ's post-resurrection appearances were hallucinatory hoaxes.

None of these five "occupied tomb" theories follow the two important principles for explaining what happened.

CHAPTER SIX

ONE THEORY
IS AS GOOD
AS ANOTHER

*"It passes the bounds of credibility that
the early Christians could have manufactured
such a tale and then preached it among those
who might easily have refuted it
simply by producing the body of Jesus."*
John Warwick Montgomery
Dean
Simon Greenleaf School of Law

*"The resurrection could not have been
maintained in Jerusalem for a single day,
for a single hour, if the emptiness of the tomb
had not been established as a fact
for all concerned."*
Paul Althaus
University of Erlangen
Germany

HISTORICAL FACT: AN EMPTY TOMB

Now, we must deal with the naturalistic explanations that are based upon the reality of an empty tomb. Quite obviously the tomb was empty on the Sunday morning after Christ's crucifixion, death and burial. The Jewish leaders have been accused of many things down through the years, but seldom has stupidity ever been one of them.

No one produced the body

The council and the high priests were both skillful dialecticians and practical politicians. They were brilliant in their handling of Pilate. Little skill would have been needed to handle Christ's followers if they knew of the location of His body. If the body of Christ was still in the tomb, when Christ's followers began preaching the resurrection, all the Jewish authorities had to do was produce the body. The disciples would have been silenced forever. Instead, the Jewish authorities forcibly brought the apostles before the Jewish council and threatened them with death if they did not immediately stop their proclaiming a risen Christ.[194] The Jews were powerless to produce Christ's body. Let's face it: They could not produce a corpse out of an empty tomb.

One must remember that Christ's enemies and the Roman security unit were the last ones to have possession of His body before the resurrection.[195]

Jewish authorities furious

Dr. Bill White is in charge of the Garden Tomb in Jerusalem which many believe to be the burial place of Christ. White observes that "the Jewish hierarchy was furious at the Apostles' preaching of the resurrection. They did all in their power to keep it from spreading, but their efforts were unavailing. If the body of Jesus still lay in the tomb where Joseph of Arimathea had placed it, what more simple and damaging refutation of the Apostles' claim than to show the populace the grave of Jesus, open it, and exhume the crucified body of this self-styled Messiah?"[196]

Beasley-Murray adds an insightful observation to the above: "It seems conveniently overlooked that the thousands of early converts to Christianity — made so through the preaching of the resurrection — were all Jews, either residents of or visitors to Jerusalem. These were accepting a revolutionary teaching which could have been discredited by taking a few minutes' walk to a garden just outside the city walls. Far from discrediting it, they one and all enthusiastically spread it far and wide. Every one of those first converts was a proof of the empty tomb, for the simple reason that they could never have become disciples if that tomb had still contained the body of Jesus."[197]

A secretary on her lunch break in downtown Jerusalem could have confirmed or denied the empty tomb. It is inconceivable that any proclamation of a risen Christ could have been maintained for a minute if both the Jews and the Christians had not been convinced that there was overwhelming evidence that the tomb was empty. The empty tomb was "too notorious to be denied." Paul Althaus states that the resurrection "could not have been maintained in Jerusalem for a single day, for a single hour, if the emptiness of the tomb had not been established as a fact for all concerned."[198]

Positive evidence

Dr. Paul Maier observes from an historical perspective that "if all the evidence is weighed carefully and fairly, it is indeed justifiable, according to the canons of historical research, to conclude that the tomb of Joseph of Arimathea, in which Jesus was buried, was actually empty on the morning of the first Easter. And no shred of evidence has yet been discovered in literary sources, epigraphy, or archaeology that would disprove this statement."[199]

As we look at the theories based upon an empty tomb, let's remember the two cardinal principles of historical investigation: (1) Any explanation needs to take into account all the facts, and (2) one must not force the evidence into a preconceived mold but rather let the facts speak for themselves.

STOLEN BY DISCIPLES

The first — and one of the most prominent — empty tomb theories is that the disciples or followers of Jesus stole the body and fabricated the resurrection story.

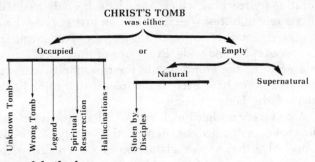

The guard bribed

This theory was even recorded by Matthew. However, it was so obviously false he didn't even bother to refute it. Matthew writes that "some of the guard came into the city and reported to the chief priests all that happened." As we saw earlier, the Roman guard went immediately to the Jewish high priest, because they knew they would have been in trouble had they gone to Pilate. They knew the Jewish rabbi had political influence over the governor, so they went there first for protection. This argues that it wasn't the Temple police who guarded the tomb. The high priest wouldn't have bribed his own men to spread a lie. He simply would have ordered, "Do it, or it's your necks."

Matthew continues, "And when they had assembled with the elders and counseled together, they gave a large sum of money to the soldiers, and said, 'You are to say, "His disciples came by night and stole Him away while we were asleep." And if this should come to the governor's ears, we will win him over and keep you out of trouble.' And they took the money and did as they had been instructed; and this story was widely spread among the Jews and is to this day."[200]

Justin, in his *Dialogue Against Trypho #108*, speaks of the story still being told: ". . . one Jesus, a Galilean deceiver, whom we crucified; but his disciples stole him by night from the tomb, where he was laid when unfastened from the cross, and now deceive men by asserting that he has risen from the dead and ascended into heaven."

This explanation of the events after the death and burial of Jesus Christ is loaded with serious problems. In fact, this feeble attempt by the Jewish authorities to stamp out the new Christian movement illustrates how desperate they were.

Would not hold up in court

The first problem with this theory is even humorous. If the Roman guard had fallen asleep, how could they have known it was "the disciples who had stolen the body"? Any lawyer for the defense would have loved to have put that captain of the guard on the stand for cross-examination. Not only would such a claim have been laughed out of court; the morning newspapers would have "crucified" the government for wasting taxpayers' money for hearing such a case.

Sleeping very improbable

The second problem is equally humorous. The mere thought that the "guard unit" would have fallen asleep must have raised some eyebrows. You'll recall in our previous discussion of the guard we saw that they were highly disciplined. Dr. George Currie, the historian, points out that a fear of punishment produced a "faultless attention to duty, especially during the night watch."[201]

This security unit was a fighting machine. If the disciples had tried anything, it would have been a "six-second war." One soldier could have dealt with the entire group of disciples. He could have single-handedly sent them running for cover. And Matthew tells us of the cowardice of the disciples. As Jesus was arrested in the garden of Gethsemane, "all the disciples left Him and fled."[202]

Roman guard would have been deaf

A third problem also has its light side. The position of the extremely large stone — moved up and away from the entire sepulcher — makes it rather difficult to defend the idea that the entire guard unit slept through it all. If the disciples had wanted to come in, tiptoe around the sleeping guards, then roll the stone over and steal the body, why did they go to the effort to move a 1-1/2-to-2-ton stone up a slope away from the entire massive sepulcher to such a position that it looked like someone had actually picked it up and carried it away?

Those soldiers would have to have had cotton in their ears with earmuffs on, not to have heard that "rolling stone." A small earthquake would have been recorded on the Richter Scale! One has to explain the position of the stone regardless of what theory you come up with.

Too honorable for deception

A fourth problem with the "theft of the body by disciples" theory is that this action would be contrary to everything written about them in history. They were men of high moral standing and honor. The historian, Edward Gibbon, in his analysis of the decline and fall of the Roman empire, points out the "purer but austere morality of the first Christians"[203] as one of the five reasons for the rapid success of Christianity.

Proponents of this theory would have to allege that the followers of Christ not only foisted a lie upon the people (a thought totally contrary to what their Master taught and died for) but that they lived out the rest of their lives proclaiming a lie about a "risen Christ." They would do all this as cowards transformed into courageous men who died as martyrs, knowing it was a deliberate fabrication.

Yet, in actuality they were willing to face arrest, imprisonment, beating, and horrible deaths, and not one of them ever denied the Lord and recanted of his belief that Christ had risen.

This is unparalleled in history. And it is even more amazing when you realize that if it were a fraud on their part, not a single one of them ever broke under pressure. Even at the point of death, they never confessed their deception to clear their consciences.

Dr. Simon Greenleaf, a famous Harvard legal authority, argued conclusively that the Apostles would have broken under pressure if Jesus Christ had not been raised from the dead.[204] The British legal authority, Dr. J.N.D. Anderson, comments that this theory "would run totally contrary to all we know of the disciples: their ethical teaching, the quality of their lives, their steadfastness in suffering and persecution. Nor would it begin to explain their dramatic transformation from dejected and dispirited escapists into witnesses whom no opposition could muzzle."[205]

This view is so far-fetched that even Dr. D.F. Strauss, a vocal opponent of Christianity, confessed, "The historian must acknowledge that the disciples firmly believed that Jesus was risen."[206] The Jewish scholar, Dr. Joseph Klausner, admits that the disciples were too honorable to perform any deception like this.[207]

For further development of the feasibility of the Apostles being martyred for a lie, see my book *More Than a Carpenter* (pp. 66-71).

The final problem with this theory needs little explanation. If the disciples had stolen Christ's body, how could the many post-resurrection appearances of Christ have been explained away — especially since they were made to over 500 people at one time?

AUTHORITIES STOLE BODY

Another similar theory is that the Roman or Jewish authorities took the body and put it in safekeeping so there could be no deception by anyone alleging a resurrection from the dead.

They would dig their own grave

This sounds good unless one stops to ask, "Why would the authorities do the very thing that caused all their problems?" The disciples went back to the very city of Jerusalem to preach, "Christ is risen." If what they were

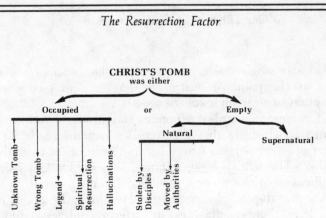

CHRIST'S TOMB
was either

Occupied   or   Empty

Natural   Supernatural

Unknown Tomb | Wrong Tomb | Legend | Spiritual Resurrection | Hallucinations | Stolen by Disciples | Moved by Authorities

teaching was false, all anyone had to do was produce the body.

Where was the official denial? Why didn't the authorities say, "That's nonsense! We gave the orders to move the body." And if that didn't suffice, why didn't they call as witnesses those who moved the body? Or why didn't they just take the doubters to the new resting place? Or show them their "storage receipt"?

As a final resort, why didn't they put the body of Christ on a carriage and march it right down the Via Dolorosa? This public display would have killed Christianity — not just in the cradle, but in the womb. There never would have been a Christianity.

There's only one reasonable answer to the above question: They couldn't produce the body. The authorities had no clue as to where it was. Christianity is a bodiless faith.

A silent alarm

Concerning the whereabouts of the body, one might conclude that "the silence of the Jews speaks louder than the voice of the Christians."[208] Dr. John Warwick Montgomery further explains, "It passes credibility that the early Christians could have manufactured such a tale, then preached it among those who might easily have refuted it simply by producing the body of Jesus."[209]

In a joking manner during a discussion on the resurrection of Christ, a Muslim student, studying in Uruguay, said to me, "You poor Christians, you don't know where you're going! We go to the tomb of our master and we have his body. You go to the tomb of your master and it's . . . ."

I noticed his bewilderment and remarked, "Go ahead, say it! It's empty!" Oh, how I would have loved to have captured his expression on a Polaroid. For the first time, this student was cognizant of the ramification of the fact that the tomb was empty.

RESUSCITATION THEORY

The next theory comes close to scraping the bottom of the barrel. It's called the "swoon theory." This view was popular with the 18th-century rationalists. Today it is popular on many university campuses and with a heterodox group of Muslims known as Ahmadiyas, though in a slightly different form.

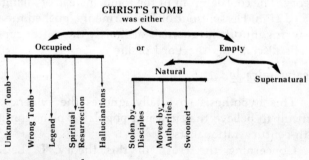

He just swoooooned

The "swoon" view goes something like this: Jesus didn't really die on the cross. It is true He was nailed to the cross and suffered from shock, pain and loss of blood. But instead of dying, He merely fainted (swooned) from exhaustion. The disciples, mistaking Him for dead, buried Him alive. They were easily misled because medical knowledge was not great at that time. The cold sepulcher in which He was placed revived Him. His disciples were so ignorant, they couldn't believe mere resuscitation revived Him, so they insisted it was a resurrection from the dead.

This theory would have to say that: (1) Jesus went through six trials — three Roman and three Jewish; (2) was beaten almost beyond description by the Roman flagrum; (3) was so weak He could not carry His own *patibulum* — the wooden cross bar; (4) had spikes driven through His hands and feet as He was crucified; (5) the Romans thrust a sword into His side and eyewitnesses said, "Blood and water came out," a sign of death; (6) four executioners confirmed His death — they must have all been mistaken; (7) 100-plus pounds of spices and a gummy substance were encased around His body — He must have breathed through it all; (8) He was put into a cold, damp tomb; (9) a large stone was lodged against its entrance; (10) a Roman guard was stationed there, and (11) a seal was placed across the entrance.

Then an incredible thing happened, according to this theory. The cool damp air of the tomb, instead of killing Him, healed Him. He split out of His garments, pushed the stone away, fought off the guards and shortly thereafter appeared to His disciples as the Lord of life.

A greater miracle

This hypothesis so totally ignores the evidence, it is difficult to believe that it was a popular explanation of the 18th-century rationalists.

Concerning the truth of this theory, E. LeCamus cleverly but very logically states: "It would be more miraculous even than the resurrection itself."[210]

A skeptic's opinion

Dr. David Strauss was one of the most bitter of all opponents of the supernatural elements in the Gospels and a man whose works did much to destroy faith in Christ. This man, despite all of his vicious criticisms and firm denials of anything partaking of the miraculous, gave the death-blow to any thought that Jesus revived from a swoon.

He said: "It is impossible that a being who has been stolen half-dead out of the sepulchre, who crept about weak and ill, wanting medical treatment; who required bandaging, strengthening and indulgence, and who still at last yielded to his sufferings, could have given to the disciples the impression that he was a Conqueror over death and the grave, the Prince of Life, an impression which lay at the bottom of their future ministry. Such a resuscitation could only have weakened the impression which He had made upon them in life and in death, at the most could only have given it an elegiac voice, but could by no possibility have changed their sorrow into enthusiasm, have elevated their reverence into worship."[211]

THE PASSOVER PLOT—PLOT

A modern twist of the swoon theory has been proposed by Hugh Schoenfield in his work, *The Passover Plot.*

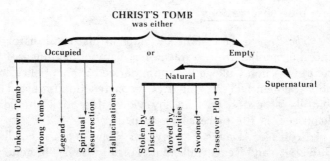

According to Schoenfield, Jesus believed He was the Messiah and therefore plotted a very timely and detailed plan to arrange what appeared to be His resurrection. Jesus took into His confidence Joseph of Arimathea, and an anonymous "young man." He knew of the many Old Testament prophecies concerning the Messiah, and ordered His life in such a manner that He could fulfill these predictions and manipulate the minds of the people.

Jesus arranged a feigned death on the cross by being administered a drug, Schoenfield said. The drug was given to Him when the wine vinegar was offered.

The plan was for Joseph to take His body to one of his tombs. When the effects of the drug wore off, Jesus would appear alive and reveal Himself as the Messiah. However, the plot was confused when, unexpectedly, the Roman guard thrust a spear into His side. He regained consciousness only temporarily and finally died. Before dawn, the mortal remains of Jesus were quickly taken away and disposed of so His grave would be empty.

The "unknown young man" then was mistaken as Jesus by an emotionally crazed Mary, Schoenfield said. On four different occasions the mysterious young man was identified as Christ by the confused disciples. Neither Joseph of Arimathea nor the "mysterious" young man ever corrected the misapprehension of the disciples. These "appearances" motivated the followers of Christ to go out and change the world.

A few plot observations

The Passover Plot is the ultimate in historical distortion and the manipulation of facts. Dr. Samuel Sandmen of the Hebrew Union College best summarized Schoenfield's creation: "Schoenfield's imaginative reconstruction is devoid of a scintilla of proof. . . . In my view, this book should be dismissed as the mere curiosity it is."[212]

Professor David Stanley, of New York's Fordham University and Regis College in Toronto, says, "In general, most of these stories belong to sensational journalism."[213]

The only reason I even mention this view is that so many students and professors make mention of it in reference to the resurrection.

The theories determine the facts

The first problem in *The Passover Plot* is Schoenfield's blatant "pick and choose" approach. It is a classic example of approaching the evidence with a preconceived theory and selecting only those facts which support your view and rejecting all others. All this is done with no apparent criteria other than how it fits with your scheme of events.

Take, for example, the guard placed at the tomb. Schoenfield rejects the guard at the tomb because Matthew was the only writer in the New Testament to record this. The reasoning seems to be, if only one writer records an event, it can be dismissed.

Schoenfield accepts the story of the thrust of the spear into Christ's side, however. In fact, it is one of the major premises in his argument.

It was the spear in Christ's side that caused Jesus' plot to fail, Schoenfield said. However, he should have rejected the story of the spear in Jesus' side since it is mentioned only in John's account.

So many problems

Other problems develop when you (1) consider the four executioners who were needed to certify the death; (2) the Roman guard for which, historically and literally, there is much evidence for its authenticity; (3) the Roman seal; (4) the size of the stone; (5) the realization that the plot would involve Jesus in a colossal hoax completely contrary to everything written about Christ in history; (6) the change in the disciples.

As Dr. J.N.D. Anderson writes of Schoenfield, "We are asked to believe that the skeptical disciples were confused by the appearance of this young man into believing that Jesus had arisen and that they were so transformed by this confusion that they turned Jerusalem upside down with their preaching."[214] And (7) with a stroke of a pen we are to eradicate all but four of the eyewitness appearances of Christ because they do not fit into the theory.

Men and women, the appeal by Paul to 500 witnesses was spoken and written at a time when the majority of those 500 were alive and could confirm or deny the reports. If there had not been 500 witnesses, Paul would have been laughed out of the synagogues and ridiculed in the theaters. Instead, thousands came to Christ in response to his preaching.

The facts speak louder than the theories

The natural theories for explaining the resurrection now have been carefully examined in light of all the

The Resurrection Factor

precautions taken at the tomb by the Roman and Jewish authorities.

Professor Paul L. Maier, a man trained to analyze historical arguments, concludes, "None of these theories, then, offers any solid base for historical reconstruction of what happened on the first Easter morning. If honestly examined, they appear quite fanciful, and all of them raise far more difficulties than they solve. No one theory explains all the phenomena reported at the time, and it would take an incredible combination of several of them to begin to do so. This much must be admitted, not merely on any basis of Christian apologetic, but of sober historical inquiry."[215]

Many times, I'm sure, the Jewish high priest must have mused, "Why did we ever ask the Romans to secure the grave?" They took so many precautions they actually overdid it and thus gave significant testimony to the resurrection of Jesus.

HE IS RISEN!

Only one conclusion takes into account all the facts and does not adjust them to preconceived notions. It is the conclusion that Christ is in fact risen — a supernatural act of God in history.

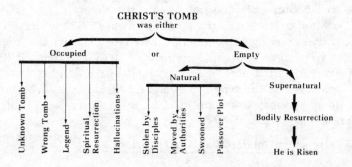

Summary

Every known historical fact (direct evidence) suggests that the tomb of Jesus Christ was empty on the third day.

Four natural theories have been advanced to explain these away:

1) The first theory weakly argues that the disciples faked the resurrection by stealing the body and went on to die martyrs' deaths for a lie.

2) The second suggests that the authorities stole the body and ignores why they didn't simply put it on display to prove that the disciples preaching Christ's resurrection were wrong.

3) The Resuscitation Theory (sometimes called the "Swoon Theory") incredibly argues that Christ was so weak from His trials and scourgings that He couldn't even carry His own cross, only appeared to die on the cross, was revived by the cool air of the tomb, shed His grave clothes, rolled back the two-ton stone, fought off the Roman guards and appeared to His disciples as the Lord of life.

4) The "Passover Plot" variation on this theory argues that Christ plotted to fulfill the prophecies about the Jewish Messiah and was only to have appeared to die on the cross. However, the unplanned spear-thrust into His side killed Him. An unknown young man was subsequently mistaken by Mary and the other disciples to be Jesus, and no one ever corrected their misapprehension.

None of these natural theories adequately deals with all the known facts surrounding the resurrection of Jesus Christ.

CHAPTER SEVEN

THE CIRCUMSTANTIAL EVIDENCE

*"That a few simple men should in one generation
have invented so powerful and appealing
a personality, so lofty an ethic,
and so inspiring a vision of human brotherhood,
would be a miracle far more incredible
than any recorded in the Gospels."*
Will Durant
Historian

There is, indeed, further evidence of Christ's bodily resurrection. It is called circumstantial evidence. "Direct evidence" deals with the fact in issue, such as, "Did Christ rise from the dead?" *The Random House Dictionary of the English Language* best conveys the meaning of "circumstantial evidence," that is, "proof of facts offered as evidence from which other facts are to be inferred."

Direct vs. circumstantial evidence

For example, in a robbery, the testimony of a witness who saw the man pull out a gun and shoot the clerk is direct evidence. But evidence that (1) the man was seen entering the story immediately before the shooting; (2) a sales slip showing he had purchased the gun; (3) his fingerprints on the gun and cash register; and (4) a ballistics report showing the bullet came from his gun — all this is circumstantial evidence.

The evidence stacks up

The inability of any one piece of circumstantial evidence to prove an ultimate fact does not make that evidence less valuable.

As McCormick points out, a brick is not a wall but small pieces of evidence do add up to a substantial proof.[216]

In a court of law, circumstantial evidence is just as valuable as direct evidence.[217] And often, strong circumstantial evidence is more trustworthy than direct evidence because it cannot be as easily fabricated.

There are six areas of circumstantial evidences that are unexplained apart from the fact of the resurrection.

CIRCUMSTANTIAL EVIDENCE #1—The Church

Fact number one is the origin and existence of the church. The early success of the Christian church is an historical phenomenon that must be explained. Its origin can be traced directly back to the city of Jerusalem in Palestine about A.D. 30. It thrived in the very city where Jesus was crucified and buried.

Do you believe for a moment that the early church could have survived for a week in its hostile surroundings if Jesus Christ had not been raised from the dead? The resurrection of its founder was preached within a few minutes' walk of Joseph's tomb. As a result of the first sermon, immediately after arguing for a risen Christ, 3,000 believed.[218] Shortly thereafter, 5,000 more believed.

Could all those converts have been made if Jesus had not been raised from the dead?

Dr. J.N.D. Anderson concludes from the evidence that the church owed its origin to the resurrection of its founder from the dead. He asks: "Is there really any other theory that fits the facts?"[219]

Dr. Daniel Fuller observes that "to try to explain this (the church) without reference to the resurrection is as hopeless as trying to explain Roman history without reference to Julius Caesar."[220]

CIRCUMSTANTIAL EVIDENCE #2—Sunday Worship

Fact number two is the sociological phenomenon of the Christian Sunday. The decision to change "the day of worship" from the Sabbath (Saturday) to the first day of the week (Sunday) probably is one of the most significant decisions ever made by a group of people in history. This is especially true when one considers the consequences the Jews believed would result if they were wrong.

The early Christians were devout Jews who were fanatical in their observance of the Sabbath. The Jews feared breaking the Sabbath. They believed they would incur the wrath of God if they broke it. Yet something happened that caused these committed Jewish men and women to turn their backs on all their years of religious training and tradition.

They changed their "day of worship" to Sunday in honor of the anniversary of the resurrection of Jesus Christ. I know of no other historical event that is celebrated 52 times a year.

The most rational explanation for all this is that Jesus Christ appeared to them after His resurrection.

CIRCUMSTANTIAL EVIDENCE #3—Baptism

A third fact is the celebration of baptism. Believers' baptism dates back to the early church. It is a public testimony by a new believer in Jesus Christ and symbolizes that at the moment of salvation, he dies with Christ in the crucifixion (going into the water) and is raised with Him in newness of life (coming out of the water) through the resurrection.

This sacrament of baptism finds its meaning in the fact of the historical resurrection of Jesus Christ.

CIRCUMSTANTIAL EVIDENCE #4—Communion

Communion is another sacrament in which the cup and bread symbolize Christ's death on the cross and the shedding of His blood for the sins of mankind. When a believer participates in communion, he acknowledges with great joy that Christ personally died for him.

How can a great joy accompany the acknowledgment of the horrifying death of his religion's founder, save the redeeming fact of a subsequent resurrection?

One of the first times I ever partook of this sacrament was at a conference in Iowa where I was the featured speaker. As they served communion, everyone was singing praises to God and were excited about his participation in it. My thoughts immediately turned to the above question, "Why so much joy over so much suffering of Christ on the cross?"

The most rational explanation is that down through the centuries the church has been convinced that Jesus Christ not only died on the cross for their sins and was buried, but that on the third day He was raised from the dead — and is alive today.

CIRCUMSTANTIAL EVIDENCE #5—Changed Lives

A fact of circumstantial evidence surrounding the resurrection of Jesus is the psychological phenomenon of transformed lives.

The Circumstantial Evidence

They had no earthly benefits

The changed lives of those early Christian believers is one of the most telling testimonies to the fact of the resurrection. We must ask ourselves: What motivated them to go everywhere proclaiming the message of the risen Christ?

Had there been visible benefits accruing to them from their efforts — such as prestige, wealth or increased social status — we might logically account for their actions. As a reward, however, for their wholehearted and total allegiance to this "risen Christ," these early Christians were beaten, stoned to death, thrown to the lions, tortured, crucified and subjected to every conceivable method of stopping them from talking. Yet they were the most peaceful of men, who physically forced their beliefs on no one. Rather they laid down their very lives as the ultimate proof of their complete confidence in the truth of their message.

Those hardest to convince

There was the skeptical family of Jesus.[221] His brothers did not believe in Him. They were embarrassed to hear their brother say to the people, "I am the way, the truth and the life, no man cometh unto the Father but by Me," and "I am the vine, you are the branches," and "I'm the shepherd, you are the sheep."[222]

What would you do if your brother did that?

There was James, His brother. He was found in the company of the Pharisees. James and his brothers mocked Jesus.

However, after Jesus went to that degrading death on the cross, disgracing the family, and was buried, where do we find those hardest to convince — His own family?

We find them in the upper room with the disciples waiting for the Holy Spirit to be sent.[223] Now, since they mocked Him while alive, what happened in a matter of a few days to turn their lives upside down?

James became a leader in the early church and wrote an epistle stating, "I James, a bond-servant of God and of the

Lord Jesus Christ (his brother). . . ."[224] Eventually (for the cause of Christ) James died a martyr's death by stoning.[225]

What happened?

The best explanation I know is recorded by Paul: ". . . then He appeared to James."[226]

His cowardly followers

What about the fearful disciples of Jesus? When the authorities captured Jesus in the Garden of Gethsemane, "all the disciples left Him and fled."[227] During Christ's trial, Peter went out and denied Him three times.[228] After Christ was crucified, the fearful disciples hid themselves in an upper room and locked the doors.[229] But something happened within days to totally change this group of cowardly followers into a bold band of enthusiasts who faced martyrdom without fear of hesitation. Peter, who had denied Jesus, was imprisoned for his persistency in preaching a "risen Christ" and later himself crucified upside down.

What happened? The most logical explanation is that "He appeared to Cephas (Peter) . . . then to all the Apostles."[230]

A Jewish fanatic converted

And how about Paul, the religious persecutor of the Christians? This Jewish fanatic so hated the followers of Christ that he obtained special permission to go to other cities and incarcerate Christ's disciples. He ravaged the church.[231]

But something happened to this persecutor. He turned from an antagonist to a protagonist of Jesus. He was transformed from a murderer to a Christian missionary. He changed from a bitter interrogator of Christians to one of the greatest propagators of the Christian faith.

The irony is that Paul began to confound the Jewish authorities "by proving Jesus is the Christ," the Son of God.[232] He was eventually killed for his devotion to Christ.

What happened? The historical explanation is Paul's statement that Jesus "appeared to me also."[233]

Paul's conversion was so dramatic, it would be the

modern equivalent of the Pope, who is world leader of the Catholic Church, becoming a Protestant.

Very little today could match the colossal event of Paul's conversion to Christianity. What Paul had thought to be lies — pure fiction — about Jesus, turned out to be undeniable fact.

It would be very difficult to explain the transformation of these men if the resurrection were not true. Professor Robert Grant says: "The origin of Christianity is almost incomprehensible unless such an event took place."[234]

A resurrection explains all the facts

Harvard law professor Simon Greenleaf, a man who lectured for years on how to break down testimony and determine whether or not a witness is lying, concludes: "It was therefore impossible that they could have persisted in affirming the truths they have narrated, had not Jesus actually risen from the dead, and had they not known this fact as certainly as they knew any other fact.

"The annals of military warfare afford scarcely an example of the like heroic constancy, patience, and un-flinching courage. They had every possible motive to review carefully the grounds of their faith, and the evidences of the great facts and truths which they asserted. . . ."[235]

Dr. George Eldon Ladd, writing of the historical signifi-cance of the change in the Apostles, says: "The historian must also admit that historical criticism has not yet found an adequate historical explanation for these facts; that for the historian the transformation in the disciples is an unsolved problem. He must also admit that the view that Jesus actually arose from the dead would explain all the facts."[236]

A believer in Jesus Christ today can have the complete confidence, as did those first Christians, that his faith is based, not on myth or legend, but on the solid historical fact of the empty tomb and the risen Christ.

He can change your life

Even more important, the individual believer can experi-ence the power of the risen Christ in his life today. First, he can know that his sins are forgiven.[237] Second, he can be assured of eternal life and his own resurrection from the grave.[238] And, third, he can be released from a meaningless and empty life and be transformed into a new creature in Jesus Christ.[239]

Summary

In a court of law, circumstantial evidence is often more trustworthy than direct evidence because it is less easily fabricated. Five points of strong circumstantial evidence argue unmistakably for the bodily resurrection of Jesus Christ:

1) The origins and existence of the Christian church are rooted in Jerusalem at the same time as it was shaken by the event of the resurrection.

2) The fact that the early Christians, all of whom were devout Jews, worshipped on Sunday instead of Saturday, the Sabbath, can be explained only because Sunday was the anniversary of the resurrection.

3) Christian water baptism which dates back to the first believers was expressly a picture of the believer being resurrected with Jesus Christ as he comes up out of the water.

4) The Christian sacrament of holy communion could not joyously celebrate the death and burial of Jesus Christ if there was not a subsequent resurrection.

5) The phenomenon of the early disciples' transformed lives cannot be explained outside the fact of the resurrection. Amid incredibly hostile conditions the disciples were immovable in their certainty about the resurrection. And the subsequent conversion and ministry of the Apostle Paul is one of the most profound transformations in all the New Testament.

CHAPTER EIGHT

HE CHANGED MY LIFE

*"I am the resurrection, and the life:
he that believeth in Me, though he were dead,
yet shall he live: and whosoever liveth
and believeth in Me shall never die."*
Jesus Christ

*"Never has Jesus had so wide and so profound
an effect upon humanity as in the past
three or four generations. Through Him
millions of individuals have been transformed
and have begun to live the kind of life
which he exemplified. . . . Gauged by
the consequences which have followed,
the birth, life, death, and resurrection of Jesus
have been the most important events in
the history of man. Measured by His influence,
Jesus is central in the human story."*
Kenneth Scott Latourette
Historian

CIRCUMSTANTIAL EVIDENCE #6—He Changed My Life

The final piece of circumstantial evidence I would like to present is what happened to me. I believe I am a walking testimony that Jesus Christ was raised from the dead and lives today. In the first chapter, I explained how I set out to intellectually refute the resurrection and Christianity. After gathering the evidence, some of which has been shared in this book, I was compelled to conclude that my arguments wouldn't stand up, that Jesus Christ was exactly who He claimed to be — the Son of God.[240]

A conflict developed

At that moment, though, I had quite a problem. My mind was telling me all this was true, but my will was pulling me in another direction. I discovered that to become a Christian is a rather ego-shattering experience.

Jesus Christ made a direct challenge to my will to trust Him. Let me paraphrase His invitation: "Look! I have been standing at the door and I am constantly knocking. If anyone hears me calling him and opens the door, I will come in."

I didn't care if He did walk on water, or turn water into wine. I didn't want a party pooper invading my life. I couldn't think of a faster way to ruin a good time.

So there I was: My mind told me Christianity was true on the one hand, and my will said, "Don't admit it." Every time I was around those enthusiastic Christians, the conflict would start again. If you've ever been around happy people when you're miserable, you understand how they can bug you. They would be so happy and I would feel so miserable I would literally get up and run right out of the student union.

It came to the point where I'd go to bed at ten at night and I wouldn't fall asleep until four in the morning. I knew I had to get Jesus off my mind or go out of my mind! I always have been open-minded, but not so open-minded that my brains could fall out.

The new life begins

Being open-minded, on December 19, 1959, at 8:30 p.m. during my second year at the university, I became a Christian.

Someone asked me, "How do you know?"

I said, "Look, I was there."

That night I prayed. I prayed four things in order to establish a relationship with the resurrected, living Christ. He since has transformed my life.

First, I said, "Lord Jesus, thank You for dying on the cross for me." Second, I said, "I confess those things in my life that aren't pleasing to You and ask You to forgive me and cleanse me." (The Bible says, "Though your sins are as scarlet they will be as white as snow.")[241] Third, I said, "Right now, in the best way I know how, I open the door of my heart and life and trust You as my Savior and Lord. Take control of my life. Change me from the inside out. Make me the type of person You created me to be."

The last thing I prayed was, "Thank You for coming into my life by faith." It was a faith based not upon ignorance but upon evidence and the facts of history and God's Word.

I'm sure you've heard religious people talk about their "bolt of lightning." Well, after I prayed nothing happened. I mean nothing. I still haven't sprouted wings! In fact, after I made that decision, I felt worse. I literally felt I was going to vomit. I felt sick deep down.

"Oh, no, McDowell, what'd you get sucked into now?" I wondered. I really felt I'd gone off the deep end — and some of my friends agreed.

The changes begin

But I can tell you one thing: In six months to a year-and-a-half, I found I hadn't gone off the deep end. My life was changed!

I was in a debate with the head of the history department at a midwestern university, and I said my life had been changed. He interrupted me with, "McDowell, are you trying to tell us that God really changed your life in the 20th century? What areas?"

After 45 minutes of my describing changes he said, "Okay, that's enough."

A mental peace

One area I told him about was my restlessness. I was a person who always had to be occupied. I had to be over at my girl's place or somewhere in a rap session. I'd walk across the campus, and my mind would be a whirlwind of conflicts. I'd sit down and try to study or think and I couldn't.

But a few months after I made that decision for Christ, a kind of mental peace began to develop. Don't misunderstand, I'm not talking about the absence of conflict. What I found in this relationship with Jesus wasn't so much the absence of conflict as it was the ability to cope with it. I wouldn't trade this for anything in the world.

A control of temper

Another area that started to change was my bad temper. I used to blow my stack if somebody just looked at me cross-eyed. I still have the scars from almost killing a man my first year in the university. My temper was such an integral part of me, I didn't consciously seek to change it.

One day, I arrived at a crisis, only to find my temper was gone! And only once in the past 21 years have I lost my temper. (But when I blew it that time, I must have made up for about six years!)

One man I hated

And there's another area of which I'm not proud. But I mention it because a lot of people need to have the same change in their lives through a relationship with the resurrected, living Christ. This is the area of hatred.

I had a lot of hatred in my life. It wasn't something outwardly manifested, but there was a kind of inward grinding. I was ticked off with people, with things, with issues. Like so many other people, I was insecure. Every time I met someone different from me, he became a threat.

The one person I hated more than anyone else in the world was my father. I despised him. To me he was the town alcoholic. If you're from a small town and one of your parents is an alcoholic, you know what I'm talking about.

Everybody knew. My friends would come to high school and make jokes about my father being downtown. They didn't think it bothered me. I was laughing on the outside, but let me tell you I was crying on the inside. I'd go out in the barn and see my mother lying in the manure behind the cows — beaten so badly she couldn't get up.

When we had friends over, I would take my father out, tie him up in the barn, and park the car up around the silo. We would tell our friends he had to go somewhere. I don't think any person could hate someone more than I hated my father.

From hatred to love

Maybe five months after I made that decision for Christ, a love from God through Jesus Christ entered my life. It took that hatred and turned it upside down. It was so strong, I was able to look my father squarely in the eyes and say, "Dad, I love you." And I really meant it. After some of the things I'd done, that shook him up.

When I transferred to a private university, I was in a serious car accident. With my neck in traction, I was taken home. I'll never forget my father coming into my room and asking, "Son, how can you love a father like me?" I said, "Dad, six months ago I despised you." Then I shared with him my conclusions about Jesus Christ.

"Dad, I let Christ come into my life," I said. "I can't explain it completely. But as a result of that relationship, I've found the capacity to love and accept not only you but other people just the way they are."

Forty-five minutes later one of the greatest thrills of my life occurred. Somebody in my own family, someone who knew me so well I couldn't pull the wool over his eyes, said to me, "Son, if God can do in my life what I've seen Him do in yours, then I want to give Him the opportunity." Right there my father prayed with me and trusted Christ.

Usually changes take place over several days, weeks, or months . . . even a year. My life was changed in about six months to a year-and-a-half. The life of my father was changed right before my eyes. It was as though somebody reached in and turned on a light bulb. I've never seen such a rapid change before or since. My father touched whiskey only once after that. He got it as far as his lips and that was it.

It works

I've come to one conclusion. A relationship with Jesus Christ changes lives. You can laugh at Christianity; you can mock and ridicule it. But it works. It changes lives. If you trust Christ, start watching your attitudes and actions, because Jesus Christ is in the business of changing lives.

It is your choice

But Christianity is not something that can be forced or shoved down someone's throat. You have your life to live, and I have mine. All I can do is tell you what I've learned. Beyond that, it's your decision. My wife puts it this way: "Because Christ was raised from the dead, He lives. And because He lives, He has that infinite capacity to enter a man or woman's life, forgive him and change him from the inside out." The key element is the resurrection factor. He is risen!

It's personal

I've shared how I personally responded to the claims of Christ. You also need to ask the logical question: "What difference does all this evidence make to me? What difference does it make whether or not I believe Christ rose again." The answer is put best by something Jesus said to Thomas. He told him: "I am the way, and the truth, and the life; no one comes to the Father but through Me."

On the basis of all the evidence for Christ's resurrection, and considering the fact that Jesus offers forgiveness of sin and an eternal relationship with God, who would be so foolhardy as to reject Him? Christ is alive! He is living today!

You can trust God right now by faith through prayer. Prayer is talking with God. God knows your heart and is not so concerned with your words as He is with the attitude of your heart. If you have never trusted Christ, you can do so right now.

The prayer I prayed is: "Lord Jesus, I need You. Thank You for dying on the cross for my sins. I open the door of my life and trust You as my Savior and Lord. Thank You for forgiving my sins and giving me eternal life. Make me the kind of person You want me to be. Thank You that I can trust You."

If you just trusted Christ, or believe you are going to do so in the near future, write me. You will have a lot of questions as I had after my decision. A professor once shared with me some principles that made sense to me about how my life could be changed through this new relationship with God through Christ. I have put these principles into letter form and would like to send them to you.

Josh McDowell
P.O. Box 5585
Richardson, TX 75080.

Summary

When the evidence forced me to the conclusion that Jesus Christ was raised from the dead and had to be, as He claimed, the Son of God, I discovered a personal problem. My mind was convinced, but my will pulled me in another direction.

On December 19, 1959, I put it all to the test by confessing Jesus Christ as Lord and asking Him to enter and to control my life. The result wasn't immediately dramatic but over the next six to eight months my life was changed.

A mental peace began to replace my restlessness. My bad temper came under control and ultimately vanished. My deep hatred for my father, the town drunk, changed to love . . . and that love changed him as he, too, prayed and trusted Christ with his life.

The same power that raised Jesus Christ from the dead is still transforming lives today. It can be yours, too, just for the asking. "Lord Jesus, I need You. Thank You for dying on the cross for me. Forgive me and cleanse me. Right this moment I trust You as Savior and Lord. Make me the type of person You created me to be. In Christ's name, amen."

APPENDIX A.

Three Days and Three Nights in the Tomb?

Many people have questioned the accuracy of Jesus' statement that "just as Jonah was three days and three nights in the belly of the sea monster, so shall the Son of Man be three days and three nights in the heart of the earth."[242] They ask, "How could Jesus have remained in the tomb three days and three nights if He was crucified on Friday and rose on Sunday?"

The accounts of His death and resurrection as given in the Gospels of Matthew, Mark, Luke and John indicate that Jesus was crucified and buried on Friday, before sundown, which is the beginning of the next day for the Jews, and resurrected on the first day of the week, which is our Sunday, before sunrise.

This puts Jesus in the grave for part of Friday, the entire Sabbath, and part of Sunday. In other words, He was in the tomb two full nights, one full day and part of two days. Since this is clearly not three full, 24-hour days, do we have a problem of conflict with the prophecy of Jesus in Matthew?[243]

Jesus is recorded as saying, "The Son of man will rise again after three days," and "He will be raised again on the third day"[244] — expressions that are used interchangeably. This can be seen from the fact that most references to the resurrection state that it occurred *on* the third day.

Also, Jesus spoke of His resurrection in John[245] stating that He would be raised up *in* three days (not the fourth day).

Matthew[246] gives weight to this idiomatic usage. After the Pharisees tell Pilate of the prediction of Jesus, "After three days I will rise again," they ask for a guard to secure the tomb until the third day.

If the phrase, "after three days," had not been interchangeable with the "third day," the Pharisees would have asked for a guard for the fourth day.

That the expression "one day and one night" was an idiom employed by the Jews for indicating a day, even when only a part of a day was indicated, can be seen also in the Old Testament.

For example, I Samuel says "For he had not eaten bread or drunk water for three days and three nights," and in the next verse, "My master left me behind . . . three days ago."[247]

Just as clearly, Genesis[248] shows this idiomatic usage. Joseph imprisoned his brothers for three days; in verse 18, he speaks to them and releases them, all on the third day.

The phrases, "after three days" and "on the third day," are not contradictory, either to each other or with Matthew[249] but simply idiomatic, interchangeable terms, clearly a common mode of Jewish expression.

Another way to look at "three days and three nights" is to take into consideration the Jewish method of reckoning time. The Jewish writers have recorded in their commentaries on the Scriptures the principle governing the reckoning of time. Any part of a period was considered a full period. Any part of a day was reckoned as a complete day. The *Babylonian Talmud* (Jewish commentaries) relates that, "The portion of a day is as the whole of it."[250]

The *Jerusalem Talmud* (so designated because it was written in Jerusalem) says, "We have a teaching, 'A day and a night are an Onah and the portion of an Onah is as the whole of it.' "[251] An *Onah* simply means, "a period of time."

The Jewish day starts at 6:00 in the evening. Dr. Custance points out that, "It is generally believed that this method of reckoning was originally based upon the fact that in the Week of Creation, the first day began with a darkness which was turned into light; and thereafter each 24-hour period is identified as 'the evening and the morning' — in this order (Gen. 1.5,8, etc.)."[252]

The "three days and three nights" in reference to Christ's period in the tomb could be calculated as follows: Christ was crucified on Friday. Any time before 6:00 p.m. Friday would be considered "one day and one night." Any time after 6:00 p.m. Friday to Saturday at 6:00 p.m. until Sunday when Christ was resurrected would be "one day and one night." From the Jewish point of view, it would make "three days and three nights" from Friday afternoon until Sunday morning.

Even today we often use the same principle in reference to time. For example: Many couples hope their child will be born before midnight December 31. If born at 11:59 p.m., the child will be treated by the IRS as being born 365 days and 365 nights of that year. This is true even if 99.9% of the year has elapsed.

The following chart visualizes the time sequence:

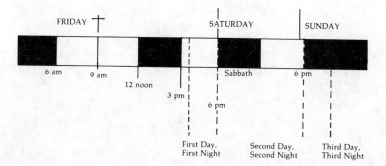

APPENDIX B.

Life of Christ in Stereo

Dr. Johnston Cheney was disturbed by the various critics' accusations about alleged contradictions in the resurrection accounts. Critics claimed inaccuracy in the women's visits to the tomb and Christ's post-resurrection appearances. Dr. Cheney spent many years composing a harmonious account of the four Gospels. He interwove all four Gospel records into one continuous account of Christ's ministry.

I have reprinted the last part of his work, *The Life of Christ in Stereo*, because of its excellent harmonizing of the post-resurrection appearances of Christ.

An earth-shaking dawn

(Mt. 28:1-15; Mk. 16:1-11; Lk. 23:56-24:12; Jn. 20:1-18)

Now when the Sabbath was past, Mary Magdalene and the other Mary, the mother of James, and Salome, bought spices that they might come and anoint him. And on the first day of the week at early dawn they came, and certain others with them, to see the sepulchre, bringing the spices and ointments which they had prepared.

And behold, there was a great earthquake; for an angel of the Lord descended from heaven, and came and rolled away the stone from the door, and sat upon it. His appearance was like lightning, and his raiment white as snow; and for fear of him those on guard trembled, and became like dead men.

[Now after Jesus rose, early on the first day of the week, he appeared first to Mary Magdalene, out of whom he had cast seven demons.] Mary came to the sepulchre while it was yet dark, and saw that the stone had been removed from the tomb. She ran therefore and came to Simon Peter, and to the other disciple, he whom Jesus loved, and said to them, "*They took away the Lord from the sepulchre! And we know not where they laid him.*"

Peter therefore and the other disciple [arose, and] went forth and ran [toward the sepulchre]. And they began to run together, but the other disciple outran Peter and reached the sepulchre first; and stooping down he saw the linen cloths lying there, but did not go in. Simon Peter therefore came following him, and he went into the sepulchre; [and stooping down], he saw the linen cloths lying [by themselves], and the napkin, which had been about his head, not lying with the linen cloths but folded up in a place by itself.

Then therefore the other disciple also, who had reached the tomb first, went in, and he saw and believed; for as yet they did not understand the scripture, that he must rise from the dead. So the disciples departed again to their abode, [wondering at what had come to pass].

"Rabboni!"

But Mary kept standing outside near the sepulchre, weeping. While therefore she was weeping, she stooped and looked into the sepulchre; and she beheld two angels in white sitting, one at the head and the other at the feet, where the body of Jesus had lain.

And they asked her, "Woman, why are you weeping?" She said to them, "*Because they took away my Lord, and I know not where they laid him.*" And when she had thus spoken, she turned around and saw Jesus standing, but did not know that it was Jesus.

Jesus said to her, "Woman, why are you weeping; whom are you seeking?" She, supposing him to be the gardener, said to him, "Sir, if *you* bore him away, tell me where you laid him, and *I* will take him away." Jesus said to her, "*Mary.*"

Turning about, she said to him, "*Rabboni!*" (which is to say, *dear Teacher!*).

Jesus said to her, "Do not hold me, for I have not yet ascended to my Father. But go to my brethren, and say to them, '*I am ascending to my Father and your Father, and to my God and your God.*' "

Mary Magdalene went and told those who had been with him, as they mourned and wept, that she had seen the Lord and he had spoken these things to her; but they, though hearing that he was *alive* and *had been seen* by her, disbelieved it.

At the tomb after sunrise

Now Joanna and Mary the mother of James and the other women with them came to the sepulchre when the sun had risen. And they were saying among themselves, "Who will roll us away the stone from the door of the sepulchre?" (For it was very great.) But when they looked up, they saw that the stone *had been* rolled away.

Then on entering the sepulchre they found not the body [of the Lord Jesus]. But it came to pass that, as they were much perplexed about this, they saw a young man sitting at the right side, clothed in a long, white garment. And they were greatly amazed; behold, *two* men stood by them in dazzling garments.

And as they became terrified and bowed their faces to the ground, the angel answered and said to the women, "Do not fear; do not be amazed. For I know that you seek Jesus of Nazareth, who was crucified. Why seek *the living* among the *dead? He is not here, for he has risen, as he said.* Remember how he spoke to you, while he was yet in Galilee, saying 'The Son of man must be delivered into the hands of sinful men, and be crucified, *and the third day rise again.*' "

And they remembered his words; and he said to them, "Come, see the place where the Lord lay. But go quickly and tell his disciples, *and Peter*, that '*He has risen from the dead, and behold, he is going before you into Galilee; there shall you see him, as he said to you*, lo, I have told you."

"Rejoice!"

So they went out quickly and fled from the sepulchre, for trembling and astonishment possessed them. Neither said they anything to anyone, for they were afraid; and they started to run to tell his disciples.

But as they were on their way, behold, *Jesus* met them, saying, *"Rejoice!"* And they came and seized him by his feet, and worshiped him. Then said Jesus to them, "Fear not; go tell my brethren to go into *Galilee*, and there shall they see me."

And they returned with great joy and told all these things to the eleven apostles, and to all the rest. But thesse words seemed to them as idle tales, and they did not believe the women.

Bribery of the guard

Now as they were going, behold, some of the guard came into the city, and reported to the chief priests all that had come to pass. And they, when they had assembled with the elders and counseled together, gave the soldiers a large sum of money, saying, "Say that *'His disciples came by night and stole him away while we slept.'* And if this comes to the governor's ears, we will 'persuade' him and free you from trouble."

So they took the money and did as they were told, and this report is spread abroad among the Jews to the present day.

Jesus and two on the Emmaus Road

(Mk. 16:12-13; Lk. 24:13-35)

[Then after these things he was revealed in another manner.] And behold, that same day two of them [were walking into the country], to a village called Emmaus, about seven miles from Jerusalem; and they were talking together about all these things that had taken place. And it came to pass that, as they conversed and reasoned, *Jesus himself* drew near and walked with them; but their eyes were held from recognizing him.

And he said to them, "What are these things which you are discussing with each other, as you walk with sad faces?" And one, whose name was Cleopas, answered and said to him, "Are *you* the only sojourner in Jerusalem who has not known the things that have happened there in recent days?"

And he asked of them, "What things?" And they said to him, "The things concerning *Jesus of Nazareth*, a man who was a prophet mighty in deed and word before God and all the people; and how the chief priests and our rulers delivered him up to be condemned to death, and crucified him. Now *we* were trusting that it was he who *would redeem Israel.*

"But to top it all, this is *the third day* since these things happened. And besides, certain women from among us astonished us, who were at the sepulchre early in the morning and did not find his body; and they came saying that they had even seen a vision of *angels,* who said that he was *alive!* And some of those who were with us went to the sepulchre and found it so, as the women had said, but him they did not see."

"Believe the prophets!"

Then said he to them, "O foolish ones, and slow of heart to believe *all* the things which the prophets uttered! *Was it not needful* that the Messiah *should suffer these things* and enter into *his glory?"* And beginning from Moses and all the prophets he expounded to them in all the Scriptures the things concerning himself.

Then they drew near to the village where they were going, and he made as though he would go farther; but they constrained him, saying, *"Lodge* with us, for it is toward evening and the day is now far spent." So he went in to lodge with them.

And it came to pass, as he reclined at table with them, that he took the bread and blessed and broke it, and began to give it to them. And their eyes were opened and they knew him; and he vanished out of their sight. Then said they to each other, "Did not our hearts burn within us, as he talked with us on the road and kept opening up to us *the Scriptures?"*

His appearance to Peter convinces

And rising up that same hour they returned to Jerusalem; and they found the eleven and those with them assembled together, saying, "*The Lord has risen indeed! And he appeared to Simon!*"

So they told the things that had happened on the road, and how he was known by them in the breaking of the bread; [but they did not believe them].

Sunday evening with the disciples

(Lk. 24:36-43; Jn. 20:19-23)

But as they were speaking these things, it being therefore evening of that first day of the week, the doors being shut where the disciples were assembled, for fear of the Jews, Jesus himself came and stood in their midst and said to them, "*Peace to you!*"

Yet they were shocked and were filled with fear, and thought that they were beholding a spirit. But he said to them, "Why are you troubled? And why do doubtings arise in your hearts? Behold my hands and my feet, that it is *I myself*. Handle me, and see; for a spirit does not have flesh and bones, as you see *I have*." And when he had said this, he showed them his hands and feet, and his side.

Then did the disciples rejoice at seeing the Lord. And while they were still disbelieving for joy and were filled with wonder, he said to them, "Have you anything here to eat?" And they gave him a piece of broiled fish and of a honeycomb, and he took and ate it before them.

Jesus therefore said again to them, "*Peace to you! As the Father has sent Me forth, so am I sending you.*" And when he had said this, he breathed on them, and said to them, "*Take the Holy Spirit. Anyone's sins which you forgive, they have been forgiven them, and anyone's sins which you retain, they have been retained.*"

The convincing of Thomas

(Jn. 20:24-29)

Now Thomas, called Didymus, one of the twelve, was not with them when Jesus came. The other disciples therefore said to him, "*We have seen the Lord!*" But he said to them, "Unless I see in his hands the imprint of the nails, and press my finger into the mark of the nails, and my hand into his side, I will *not at all believe.*"

Then after eight days his disciples were again indoors, and Thomas with them. Though the doors had been shut, Jesus came and stood in their midst, and said "*Peace to you!*"

Then said he to Thomas, "Bring here your finger and look at my hands, and bring your hand and press it into my side, and be not unbelieving but *believing.*" And Thomas answered and said to him, "*My Lord and my God!*" Jesus said to him, "Because you have seen me, Thomas, you have believed; blessed are they who have *not* seen and yet have believed."

With seven disciples in Galilee

(Jn. 21:1-24)

After these things Jesus revealed himself to the disciples again, this time at the Sea of Tiberias, and he did so in this way.

There were together Simon Peter and Thomas called Didymus and Nathanael of Cana of Galilee, and the sons of Zebedee and two others of his disciples. Simon Peter said to them, "I am going *fishing.*" They said to him, "We also are going with you." They went out at once and climbed into the boat. But that night they caught nothing.

But when morning had now come, Jesus was standing on the shore, though the disciples did not know that it was Jesus. So Jesus said to them, "Children, have you anything to eat?" They replied to him, "No." And he said to them, "Cast out the net on the *right* side of the boat, and you will find some." So they cast it, and now they could not draw it in for the size of the haul.

That disciple whom Jesus loved said therefore to Peter, "*It is the Lord!*" So when Simon Peter heard that it was the Lord, he thrust his coat around him, for he was naked, and flung himself into the sea. And the other disciples came in the small ship (for they were not far from shore, perhaps a hundred yards) dragging the net filled with fish.

"Come to breakfast"

When therefore they got out on shore, they saw a fire of coals that had been laid there, and fish placed upon it, and bread. Jesus said to them, "Bring some of the fish you have just caught." Simon Peter went on board and drew the net to shore, filled with one hundred fifty-three large fish. And in spite of there being so many the net was not torn.

Jesus said to them, "Come; *have breakfast.*" But not one of the disciples dared ask him, "Who are *you?*" For they knew that it was the Lord. Jesus therefore came and took the bread and gave to them, and likewise of the fish. This was now the third time that Jesus was revealed to his disciples after he was raised from the dead.

"Do you love me, Simon?"

When therefore they had eaten breakfast, Jesus said to Simon Peter, "Simon, son of John, do you *love* me, *more than these?*" He said to him, "Yes, Lord; *You* know my *affection* for You." He said to him, "*Feed My lambs.*"

Again a second time he said to him, "Simon, son of John, *do* you *love* me?" He said to him, "*Yes,* Lord! *You* know my *affection* for You." He said to him, "*Shepherd My sheep.*"

He said to him the third time, "Simon, son of John, do you *have affection* for me?" Peter was *grieved* because of the third question, "Do you *have affection* for me?" and he said to him, "Lord, *You* know *all things: You know* that I *have affection* for You!"

Jesus said to him, "*Feed My sheep!* Verily, verily, I say to you, when you were younger, you girded yourself and walked where you desired; but when you are old, you will stretch out your hands and another will gird you and carry you where you would not go." Now this he said to signify by what death he would glorify God. And when he had spoken this, he said to him, "*Follow Me.*"

The story told by John closes

But Peter turned about and saw following them the disciple whom Jesus loved, who also at the supper had leaned against his breast and said, "Lord, *who* is he that betrays You?" At seeing him Peter said to Jesus, "But what of *this* man, Lord?" Jesus said to him, "If I desire that he remain *till I come*, what is it to *you? Follow Me!*"

Therefore the saying spread abroad among the brethren that that disciple would not die; yet Jesus did not tell him that he would not die, but said, "If I desire that he remain *till I come*, what is it to *you?*" He is the disciple who testifies of these things and wrote these things, and we know that his testimony is true.

On a mountain in Galilee

(Mt. 28:16-20)

Then the eleven disciples proceeded into Galilee to the mountain to which Jesus had directed them. And when they saw him, they worshiped him, though some doubted.

And Jesus came to them and addressed them, saying, *"All authority has been given unto Me in heaven and upon earth. Go therefore and disciple all the nations, baptizing them in the name of the Father and of the Son and of the Holy Spirit, teaching them to observe everything I commanded you. And lo, I am with you always, until the consummation of the age."*

His final appearing and ascension

(Mk. 16:14-20b; Lk. 24:44-53)

[Afterward he was manifested to the eleven as they were reclining at table; and he reproached their unbelief and hardness of heart, because they had not believed those who saw him after he had risen.

And he said to them, *"Go into all the world and proclaim the Glad News to the whole creation. He who believes and is baptized shall be saved, but he who disbelieves shall be condemned.*

"And these *miraculous signs* will accompany those who believe: in My name will they cast out demons; they will speak in new tongues; they will pick up serpents; and if they drink any deadly thing, it will not in any way hurt them; they will lay hands on the sick and they will recover."

Parting words to the eleven

And he said to them, "These are the words which I spoke to you while I was yet with you: that *all things must be fulfilled which have been written in the law of Moses and the prophets and the psalms concerning me.*"

Then opened he their understanding that they might comprehend the Scriptures, and said to them, "*Thus it has been written, and so it was needful, that the Messiah should suffer and rise from the dead on the third day; and that repentance and remission of sins should be proclaimed in his name to all the nations, beginning at Jerusalem.*

"*And you are witnesses of these things. And behold, I am sending forth the promise of my Father upon you. But remain in the city of Jerusalem till you are clothed with power from on high.*"

He ascends from the Mount of Olives

So then the Lord Jesus, after speaking thus to them, led them out as far as to Bethany; and he lifted up his hands and blessed them. And it came to pass that, as he was blessing them, he was parted from them [and was carried up into heaven, and sat at the right hand of God].

And they [worshiped him, and] returned to Jerusalem with great joy and were continually in the temple, praising and blessing God. [And they went forth and preached everywhere, the Lord working with them and confirming the message by the miraculous signs that followed.]

That you may have life

(Jn. 21:25; 20:30-31)

Now Jesus also wrought in the presence of his disciples many other miraculous signs which are not written in this book; if they were written one by one, I suppose that not even the world itself could contain the books that would be written.

But these have been written *that you may believe that* Jesus is THE MESSIAH, THE SON OF GOD, and *that believing you may have life in His name.*

(Cheney, Johnston M., *The Life of Christ in Stereo*, Portland, Western Baptist Seminary Press, 1969, pp. 204-214.)

APPENDIX C.

The Trial of Jesus

One of the finest works ever published on the legal aspects of the trial, crucifixion and resurrection of Jesus Christ is the two-volume series, *The Trial of Jesus*, by Walter M. Chandler, former justice of the New York State Supreme Court. (Another authoritative source on the trial is Josef Blinzler's *The Trial of Jesus*.)

Chandler's treatment on evaluating a witness's testimony is extremely valuable. It is an excellent source for analyzing the accuracy of the New Testament resurrection accounts. The author believes this material will greatly enhance the reader's understanding of the facts surrounding Christ's resurrection:

The credit due to the testimony of witnesses depends upon, first, their honesty; secondly, their ability; thirdly, their number and the consistency of their testimony; fourthly, the conformity of the testimony with experience; and fifthly, the coincidence of their testimony with collateral circumstances.

Let us apply these successive tests, in the order above enumerated, to the Evangelists.

(1) In the first place, let us consider the question of their *honesty*.

The meaning of the word "honesty," used in this connection, is peculiar. It relates rather to personal sincerity than to personal integrity, and suggests the idea of perjury rather than theft in criminal law. Were the witnesses honest? That is, were they sincere? Did they intend to tell the truth? That is, did they themselves believe what they testified? If so, they were honest witnesses, though their testimony was false, as a result of error in judgment or mistake of fact.

In the sense, then, of *sincerity* is the test of honesty to be applied to the Evangelists as witnesses of the facts which they relate in the New Testament narratives. And in making this test let us bear in mind the nature and scope of this work; that it is not a religious treatise, and that the question of inspiration must not be allowed to confuse a purely legal and historical discussion. As secular historians, and not as inspired writers, must the Evangelists be considered. And in testing their credibility, the customary standards employed in analyzing the motives and conduct of ordinary men in the usual experiences and everyday affairs of life must be applied. To regard them as strange or supernatural beings, subject to some awful influence, and acting under the guidance and protection of some god or hero, is decidedly foreign to the present purpose.

It is felt that only two considerations are needed in applying the test of sincerity to the Evangelists: (1) Character; (2) Motive. And this for the reason that honest character and righteous motive are the legitimate parentage of perfect sincerity. Then, as a primary consideration, in discussing their sincerity, it may be reasonably contended that the Gospel writers were either good men or bad. A middle ground is not possible in their case, since the issues joined and the results attained were too terrible and stupendous to have been produced by negative or indifferent forces. Were they good men, then they believed what they taught and wrote, and were sincere, else they deliberately palmed off an imposture on the world, which is inconsistent with the hypothesis that they were good. Were they bad men, then their lives and teachings furnish a contradiction in principle and an inversion in the nature and order of cause and effect which history has not elsewhere recorded, either before or since; for, in their discourses and their writings, they portrayed the divinest character and proclaimed the sublimest truths known to the children of men. Every serious, thoughtful mind at once inquires: Could bad men, conspirators and hypocrites, have painted such a character — one whose perfect purity and sinless beauty mock and shame the mental and spiritual attributes of every false prophet and of all heathen gods? The Olympian Zeus, the sovereign creation of the superb Greek intellect, was a fierce and vindictive deity — at times a faithless spouse and a drunken debauchee. Mahomet, whom two hundred millions of the human race worship as the Inspired of Allah, was cruel and treacherous in warfare, and base and sensual in private life. The Great Spirit of the Indian granted immortality to dogs, but denied it to women. Other hideous and monstrous attributes deformed the images and blurred the characters of pagan prophets and heathen divinities. But Jesus of Nazareth was a pure and perfect being who claimed to be sinless,[253] and whose claims have been admitted by all the world, believers and unbelievers alike. The great truths taught by the gentle Nazarene and transmitted by the Evangelists have brought balm and healing to the nations, have proclaimed and established universal brotherhood among men. Is it probable that such a character was painted and such truths proclaimed by dishonest and insincere men? Can Vice be the mother of Virtue? "Do men gather grapes of thorns or figs of thistles?" If Jesus was not really the pure and holy being portrayed by the Gospels, then the Evangelists have created a sublime character in a superb fiction which surpasses anything to be found in profane literature, and that evil-minded men could neither have conceived nor executed. It is impossible to derive from these reflections any other conclusion than the absolute honesty and perfect sincerity of the Evangelists. Besides, the mere perusal of their writings leaves a deep impression that they were pure and pious men.

Again, a second and more serious consideration than that of character, as affecting the sincerity of the Gospel writers, is the question of motive. If the Evangelists were insincere and did not believe their own story, what motive prompted them to tell it, to preach it, and to die for it? It is not believed that all men are now or have ever been wholly selfish, but it is contended that desire for compensation is the main inducement to human action, mental and manual. Reward is the great golden key that opens the door of the Temple of Labor, and some form of recompense, here or hereafter, explains all the bustling activity of men. The Apostles themselves acted in obedience to this law, for we find them quarreling among themselves as to place and precedence in the New Kingdom. They even demanded of the Master the exact nature of their reward for labors performed and sacrifices endured. To which reply was made that they should sit on twelve thrones and judge the Twelve Tribes of Israel.

Now let us apply this principle of expectation of reward to the conduct of the Evangelists in preaching and publishing the Gospel of the Nazarene, and let us note particularly the result as it affects the question of motive in human conduct. But first let us review, for a moment, the political and religious situation at the beginning of the Apostolic ministry. The Master and Savior of the first Christians had just perished as a malefactor on the cross. The religion which the Apostles began to preach was founded in the doctrine of repentance from sins, faith in the Crucified One, and belief in His resurrection from the dead. Christianity, of which these elements were the essentials, sought to destroy and supplant all other religions. No compromises were proposed, no treaties were concluded. The followers of the Nazarene raised a black flag against paganism and every heathen god. No quarter was asked and none was given. This strange faith not only defied all other religions, but mocked all earthly government not built upon it. The small, but devoted, band, thus arrayed against themselves in the very beginning all the opposing religious and secular forces of the earth. Judaism branded the new creed as a disobedient and rebellious daughter. Paganism denounced it as a sham and a fraud, because its doctrines were unknown to the Portico and the Academy, and because its teachings were ridiculed by both Stoics and Epicureans. The Roman State cast a jealous and watchful eye upon the haughty pretensions of a religious system that taught the impotence of kings and sought to degrade earthly royalty.

The Trial of Jesus

In seeking, then, to establish the new faith and to inculcate its doctrines, what could and did the Evangelists expect but the bitter opposition which they met? Did they seriously hope to see the proud and haughty Sadducee, who despised the common people, or the kingly aristocracy of Rome, that vaunted a superhuman excellence, complacently accept a religion that taught the absolute equality and the universal brotherhood of men? Did they not expect what they actually received — bitter persecution, horrible torture, and cruel death? Then we are led to ask: Was this the recompense which they sought? Again, we pose the question: What was the motive of these men in thus acting, if they were dishonest and insincere? If they knew that they were preaching a falsehood, what reward did they expect? Was it of an earthly or a heavenly kind? It is unreasonable to suppose that they looked forward to earthly recompense when their teachings arrayed against them every spiritual and temporal potentate who had honors to grant or favors to confer. Were they looking for heavenly reward? It is ridiculous to imagine that they hoped to gain this by preaching a falsehood in this world. Nothing could be, therefore, more absurd than the proposition that a number of men banded themselves together, repudiated the ancient faith of their fathers, changed completely their mode of life, became austere in professing and practicing principles of virtue, spent their entire lives proclaiming certain truths to mankind, and then suffered the deaths of martyrs — all for the sake of a religion which they knew to be false. If they did not believe it to be false, they were sincere, and one element of their credibility is established. It is not a question at this time as to the absolute correctness of their statements. These statements might have been false, though their authors believed them to be true — it is a question of sincerity at this point; and the test of sincerity, as an element of credibility, rests upon the simple basis that men are more disposed to believe the statement of a witness if it is thought that the witness himself believes it.

(2) In the second place, let us consider the *ability* of the Evangelists as a test of their credibility as witnesses.

The text writers on the Law of Evidence are generally

agreed that the ability of a witness to speak truthfully and accurately depends upon two considerations: (1) His natural powers of observation, which enable him to clearly perceive, and his strength of memory, which enables him to fully retain the matters of fact to which his testimony relates; (2) his opportunities for observing the things about which he testifies.

To what extent the Gospel writers possessed the first of these qualifications — that is, power of observation and strength of memory — we are not informed by either history or tradition. But we are certainly justified in assuming to be true what the law actually presumes: that they were at least men of sound mind and average intelligence. This presumption, it may be remarked, continues to exist in favor of the witness until an objector appears who proves the contrary by competent and satisfactory evidence. It is not believed that this proof has ever been or can ever be successfully established in the case of the Evangelists.

Aside from this legal presumption in their favor, there are certain considerations which lead us to believe that they were well qualified to speak truthfully and authoritatively about the matters relating to Gospel history. In the first place, the writings themselves indicate extraordinary mental vigor, as well as cultivated intelligence. The Gospels of Luke and John, moreover, reveal that elegance of style and lofty imagery which are the invariable characteristics of intellectual depth and culture. The "ignorant fishermen" idea is certainly not applicable to the Gospel writers. If they were ever very ignorant, at the time of the composition of the Evangelical writings they had outgrown the affliction. The fact that the Gospels were written in Greek by Hebrews indicates that they were not entirely illiterate.

Again, the occupations of two of them are very suggestive. Matthew was a collector at the seat of customs,[254] and Luke was a physician.[255] Both these callings required more than ordinary knowledge of men, as well as accurate powers of observation, discrimination, and analysis.

But it has been frequently urged that, regardless of their natural endowments, the Evangelists were biased in favor of

Jesus and His teachings, and bitterly prejudiced against all opposing faiths. In other words, they were at the same moment both enthusiasts and fanatics. For this reason, it is contended, their testimony is unreliable. This is without doubt the weakest assault ever made upon the trustworthiness of the Gospel narratives. That the Gospel writers were neither fanatics nor enthusiasts is evident from the very tone and style of the Sacred Writings themselves. The language of fanaticism and enthusiasm is the language of rant and rage, of vituperation and of censure, on the one hand, and of eulogy and adulation on the other. The enthusiast knows no limit to the praise of those whose cause he advocates. The fanatic places no bounds to his denunciation of those whom he opposes. Now, the most remarkable characteristic of the New Testament histories is the spirit of quiet dignity and simple candor which everywhere pervades them. There is nowhere the slightest trace of bitterness or resentment. There is enthusiasm everywhere in the sense of religious fervor, but nowhere in the sense of unbecoming heat or impatient caviling. The three eventful years of the ministry of Jesus afforded many opportunities for the display of temper and for the use of invective in the Evangelical writings. The murder of the Baptist by Herod; his cunning designs against Jesus; the constant dogging of the footsteps of the Master by the spies of the Sanhedrin; and His crucifixion by the order of Pontius Pilate — what more could be desired to make the heart rage and the blood boil? But nowhere is there the slightest exhibition of violent feeling or extravagant emotion. A gentle forbearance, a mild equanimity, a becoming dignity, mark every thought and utterance. The character of Pilate, as portrayed in the New Testament, is a supreme illustration of the fairness and magnanimity of the Gospel writers. Philo and Josephus describe the Roman procurator as stubborn, cruel, and vindictive. The only kindly suggestion touching the character of Pilate that has come down from the ancient world, is that contained in the writings of men who, above all others, would have been justified in describing him as cowardly and craven. Instead of painting him as a monster, they have linked conscience to his character and stored mercy in his heart, by their accounts of his repeated attempts to release Jesus. Fanatics and enthusiasts would not have done this.

Again, the absence of both bias and prejudice in the minds and hearts of the Evangelists is shown by the fact that they did not hesitate to record their own ludicrous foibles and blunders, and to proclaim them to the world. A disposition to do this is one of the surest indications of a truthful mind. It is in the nature of "a declaration against interest," in the phraseology of the law; and such declarations are believed because it has been universally observed that "men are not likely to invent anecdotes to their own discredit." "When we find them in any author," says Professor Fisher in his "Grounds of Theistic and Christian Belief," "a strong presumption is raised in favor of his general truthfulness." Many passages of New Testament Scriptures place Jesus and the Apostles in a most unfavorable light before the world. The denial of the Master by Peter[256] and His betrayal by Judas;[257] the flight of the Eleven from the Garden at the time of the arrest;[258] the ridiculous attempt of Peter to walk upon the sea and his failure because of lack of faith;[259] the frequent childish contentions among the disciples for place and precedence in the affections of Jesus and in the New Kingdom;[260] the embassy from John the Baptist to Jesus asking if He, Jesus, was the Messiah, after the latter had already visited the former, and had been baptized by him;[261] the belief of the family of Jesus that He was mad;[262] and the fact that His neighbors at Nazareth threatened to kill Him by hurling Him from a cliff[263] — these various recitals have furnished a handle to skeptical criticism in every age. They might as well have been omitted from the Gospel histories; and they would have been omitted by designing and untruthful men.

Again, touching the question of bias and prejudice, it is worthy of observation that skeptics fail to apply the same rules of criticism to sacred that they employ in profane literature. It is contended by them that the Evangelists are unworthy of belief because their writings record the words and deeds of their own Lord and Master. It is asserted that this sacred and tender relationship warped and blinded their judgment, and disqualified them to write truthfully the facts and circumstances connected with the life and ministry of the founder of their faith. But these same critics do not apply the same tests of credibility to secular writers sustaining similar relationships. The Commentaries of Caesar and the Anabasis of Xenophon record the mighty deeds and brilliant achievements of their authors; but this fact does not destroy their reliability as historical records in the estimation of those who insist that the Gospel writers shall be rejected on grounds of bias and partiality. The Memorabilia of Xenophon, "Recollections of Socrates," is the tribute of an affectionate and admiring disciple; and yet, all the colleges and universities in the world employ this work as a text-book in teaching the life and style of conversation of the great Athenian philosopher. It is never argued that the intimate relationship existing between Xenophon and Socrates should affect the credibility of the author of the Memorabilia. The best biography in the English language is Boswell's "Life of Johnson." Boswell's admiration for Dr. Johnson was idolatrous. At times, his servile flattery of the great Englishman amounted to disgusting sycophancy. In spite of this, his work is a monumental contribution to historical literature. The "Encyclopedia Britannica" says that "Boswell has produced the best biography the world has yet seen;" but why not reject this book because of its author's spaniel-like devotion to the man whose life he has written? If Matthew, Mark, Luke, and John are to be repudiated on the ground of bias, why not repudiate Caesar, Xenophon, and Boswell? It is respectfully submitted that there is no real difference in logic between the tests of credibility applicable to sacred, and those required in the case of profane writers. A just and exact criticism will apply the same rules to both.

As to the second qualification above mentioned, under the second legal test of credibility laid down by Starkie, that is, the opportunity of observing facts and circumstances about which testimony is given, it may safely be said that the majority of the Evangelists possessed it in the highest degree. The most convincing testimony that can possibly be offered in a court of law is that of an eyewitness who has seen or heard what he testifies. Now, it is reasonably certain that all of the Gospel writers were eyewitnesses of most of the events recorded by them in the Gospel histories. Both Matthew and John were numbered among the Twelve who constantly attended the Master in all His wanderings, heard His discourses, witnessed the performance of His miracles, and proclaimed His faith after He was gone. It is very probable that Mark was another eyewitness of the events in the life and ministry of the Savior. It is now very generally agreed that the author of the Second Gospel was the young man who threw away his garment and fled at the time of the arrest in the Garden.[264] If Mark was actually present at midnight in Gethsemane peering through the shadows to see what would be done to the Nazarene by the mob, it is more than probable that he was also a witness of many other events in the life and ministry of the great Teacher. But, whether this be true or not, it is very well settled that the Second Gospel was dictated to Mark by Peter, who was as familiar with all the acts and words of Jesus as was Matthew or John. The Christian writers of antiquity unanimously testify that Mark wrote the Gospel ascribed to him, at the dictation of Peter. If their testimony is true, Peter is the real author of the Second Gospel. That the Gospel of Mark was written by an eyewitness is the opinion of Renan, the skeptic, who says: "In Mark, the facts are related with a clearness for which we seek in vain amongst the other Evangelists. He likes to report certain words of Jesus in Syro-Chaldean. He is full of minute observations, coming doubtless from an eye-witness. There is nothing to prevent our agreeing with Papias in regarding this eye-witness, who evidently had followed Jesus, who had loved Him and observed Him very closely, and who had preserved a lively image of Him, as the Apostle Peter himself."[265] The same writer declares Matthew to have been an eyewitness of the events described by him. He says: "On the whole, I admit as authentic the four canonical Gospels. All, in my opinion, date from the first century, and the authors are, generally speaking, those to whom they are attributed; but their historic value is diverse. Matthew evidently merits an unlimited confidence as to the discourses; they are the Logia, the identical notes taken from a clear and lively remembrance of the teachings of Jesus."

That Luke was an eyewitness of many of the things recorded by him, and that the others were related to him by eyewitnesses, is perfectly clear from the introductory verses of his Gospel. In addressing his royal patron, Theophilus, he assures him that those who communicated the information contained in the Gospel to him were eyewitnesses; and follows by saying that he himself had had "perfect understanding of all things from the very first."[266] The evident meaning of this is that, desiring full information for Theophilus, he had supplemented his own personal knowledge by additional facts secured from eyewitnesses to those things which, not being of the Twelve, he himself had not seen.

St. John was peculiarly well qualified to record the sayings and doings of the Christ. He was called "the disciple whom Jesus loved." He was admitted into the presence of the Savior, at all times, on terms of the utmost intimacy and friendship. At the Last Supper, his head reposed confidingly and lovingly upon the bosom of the Master. Together with Peter and James, he witnessed the resurrection of Jairus' daughter; was present at the Transfiguration on the Mount, and at the agony of the Savior in the Garden. From the cross, Jesus placed upon him the tender and pathetic burden of caring for His mother; and, running ahead of Peter, he was the first among the Twelve to arrive at the open sepulchre. By means of a favorable acquaintanceship with the High Priest, he was enabled to gain access to the palace and to be present at the trial of Jesus, as well as to introduce Peter, his friend.

It is thus clearly evident that the Evangelists were amply able, from any point of view, to truthfully and accurately record the events narrated in the Gospel histories. As eyewitnesses, being on the ground and having the situation well in hand, they were certainly better qualified to write truthful history of the events then occurring than historians and critics who lived centuries afterwards.

But it is frequently contended that, if the Evangelists were eyewitnesses of the leading events which they recorded, they committed them to writing so long afterwards that they had forgotten them, or had confused them with various traditions that had in the meantime grown up. There may be some little truth in this contention, but not enough to destroy the credibility of the witnesses as to events such as the Crucifixion and Resurrection of Jesus. These are not matters to be easily forgotten or confused with other things. The date of the composition and publication of the different Gospels is not known. But Professor Holtzmann, of Heidelberg (a man who cannot be said to be favorable to Christianity, since he was for several years the leader of the freethinkers in the Grand Duchy of Baden), after many years of careful study of the subject, declared that the Synoptic Gospels, the first three, were committed to writing between the years 60 and 80 of our era.[267] This was only from thirty to fifty years after the death of Jesus. Could men of average memory and intelligence who had been almost daily preaching the life and deeds of Jesus during these thirty or fifty years have forgotten them? The testimony of Principal Drummond, of Oxford, is very pertinent at this point. He says: "If we suppose that the Synoptic Gospels were written from forty to sixty years after the time of Christ, still they were based on earlier material, and even after forty years the memory of characteristic sayings may be perfectly clear. . . . I have not a particularly good memory, but I can recall many sayings that were uttered forty, or even fifty, years ago, and in some cases can vividly recollect the scene."[268]

If the Evangelists were eyewitnesses, which the records seem clearly to indicate, they possessed one of the strongest tests of credibility.

(3) In the third place, as to their *number* and the *consistency* of their testimony.

The credibility of a witness is greatly strengthened if his testimony is corroborated by other witnesses who testify to substantially the same thing. The greater the number of supporting witnesses, fraud and collusion being barred, the greater the credibility of the witness corroborated. But corroboration implies the presence in evidence of due and reasonable consistency between the testimony of the witness testifying and that of those corroborating. A radical discrepancy on a material point not only fails to strengthen, but tends to destroy the credibility of one or both the witnesses.

Now, the fierce fire of skeptical criticism during all the ages has been centered upon the so-called discrepancies of the Gospel narratives. It is asserted by many or a sudden change in the position of one or both the parties, causing distraction of attention, at the time of the occurrence of the events involved in litigation — all or any of these conditions, as well as many others, may create discrepancies and contradictions where there is a total absence of any intention to misrepresent. A thorough appreciation of this fact will greatly aid in a clear understanding of this phase of the discussion.

Again, an investigation of the charge of discrepancy against the Gospel writers shows that the critics and skeptics have classified mere *omissions* as contradictions. Nothing could be more absurd than to consider an omission a contradiction, unless the requirements of the case show that the facts and circumstances omitted were essential to be stated, or that the omission was evidently intended to mislead or deceive. Any other contention would turn historical literature topsy-turvy and load it down with contradictions. Dion Cassius, Tacitus, and Suetonius have all written elaborately of the reign of Tiberius. Many things are mentioned by each that are not recorded by the other two. Are we to reject all three as unreliable historians because of this fact? Abbott, Hazlitt, Bourrienne, and Walter Scott have written biographies of Napoleon Bonaparte. No one of them has recited all the facts recorded by the others. Are these omissions to destroy the merits of all these writers and cause them to be suspected and rejected? Grafton's Chronicles rank high in English historical literature. They comprise the reign of King

John; and yet make no mention of the granting of Magna Charta. This is as if the life of Jefferson had been written without mention of the Declaration of Independence; or a biography of Lincoln without calling attention to the Emancipation Proclamation. Notwithstanding this strange omission, Englishmen still preserve Grafton's Chronicles as valuable records among their archives. And the same spirit of generous criticism is everywhere displayed in matters of profane literature. The opponents of Christianity are never embarrassed in excusing or explaining away omissions of contradictions, provided the writer is a layman and his subject secular. But let the theme be a sacred one, and the author an ecclesiastic — preacher, priest, or prophet — and immediately incredulity rises to high tide, engulfs the reason, and destroys all dispassionate criticism. Could it be forgotten for a moment that Matthew, Mark, Luke, and John were biographers of the Christ, a sacred person, no difficulties would arise in the matter of inconsistencies, no objections would be made to their credibility. The slight discrepancies that undoubtedly exist would pass unnoticed, or be forever buried under the weight of an overwhelming conviction that they are, in the main, accurate and truthful.

But the Evangelists were guided by inspiration, the skeptics say; and discrepancies are inconsistent with the theory of inspiration. God would not have inspired them to write contradictory stories. But the assumption is false that they claimed to be guided by inspiration; for, as Marcus Dods truthfully says, "none of our Gospels pretends to be infallible or even *inspired*. Only one of them tells us how its writer obtained his information, and that was by careful inquiry at the proper sources."[269]

But whether the Gospel writers were inspired or not is immaterial so far as the purpose of this chapter is concerned. The rules of evidence testing their credibility would be the same in either case.

A more pertinent observation upon the Gospel discrepancies has not been made than that by Paley in his "Evidences of Christianity," where he says:

The Trial of Jesus

I know not a more rash or more unphilosophical conduct of the understanding than to reject the substance of a story by reason of some diversity in the circumstances with which it is related. The usual character of human testimony is substantial truth under circumstantial variety. This is what the daily experience of courts of justice teaches. When accounts of a transaction come from the mouths of different witnesses it is seldom that it is not possible to pick out apparent or real inconsistencies between them. These inconsistencies are studiously displayed by an adverse pleader, but oftentimes with little impression upon the minds of the judges. On the contrary, a close and minute agreement induces the suspicion of confederacy and fraud. When written histories touch upon the same scenes of action, the comparison almost always affords ground for a like reflection. Numerous, and sometimes important, variations present themselves; not seldom, also, absolute and final contradictions; yet neither one nor the other are deemed sufficient to shake the credibility of the main fact. The embassy of the Jews to deprecate the execution of Claudian's order to place his statue in their temple, Philo places in the harvest, Josephus in seed-time; both contemporary writers. No reader is led by this inconsistency to doubt whether such an embassy was sent, or whether such an order was given. Our own history supplies examples of the same kind. In the account of the Marquis of Argyll's death, in the reign of Charles II, we have a very remarkable contradiction. Lord Clarendon relates that he was condemned to be hanged, which was performed the same day; on the contrary, Burnet, Woodrow, Heath, Echard, concur in stating that he was condemned upon the Saturday and executed upon a Monday. Was any reader of English history ever skeptic enough to raise from hence a question, whether the Marquis of Argyll was executed or not? Yet this ought to be left in uncertainty, according to the principles upon which the Christian history has sometimes been attacked.[270]

The reader should most carefully consider the useful as well as the damaging effect of Gospel inconsistencies in the matter of the credibility of the Evangelists. A certain class of persons have imagined the Gospel writers to be common conspirators who met together at the time and place to devise ways and means of publishing a false report to the world. This is a silly supposition, since it is positively known that the authors of the Evangelical narratives wrote and published them at different times and places. Moreover, the style and contents of the books themselves negative the idea

The Resurrection Factor

of a concerted purpose to deceive. And, besides, the very inconsistencies themselves show that there was no "confederacy and fraud;" since intelligent conspirators would have fabricated exactly the same story in substantially the same language.

Furthermore, a just and impartial criticism will consider not only the discrepant but also the corroborative elements in the New Testament histories. It should not be forgotten that the authors of the Gospels were independent historians who wrote at different times and places. Then, in all matters of fact in which there is a common agreement, they may be said to fully corroborate each other. And it may be contended without fear of successful contradiction that, when so considered, there will be found numerous cases of corroboration where there is one of discord or inconsistency.

The corroborative elements or features in the Evangelical narratives may be classified under three headings: (1) Instances in which certain historical events related by one of the Gospel writers are also told by one or more of the others. These are cases of ordinary corroboration. (2) Instances in which the recital of a certain fact by one of the Evangelists would be obscure or meaningless unless explained or supplemented by another. These may be regarded as examples of internal confirmation. (3) Instances in which the fact related by one Evangelist must be true from the nature of the case, regardless of what the others have said. This is the simple confirmation of logic or reason.

A few illustrations will serve to make clear this classification.

Under the first heading of "ordinary corroboration" may be mentioned the accounts of the miracle of feeding the five thousand. All the Evangelists tell us of this event, and each records the fact that the fragments taken up were *twelve baskets full.*[271]

Under the second heading of "internal confirmation" the following instances may be cited:

Matt. xxvi. 67, 68: "And others smote him with the palms of their hands, saying, Prophesy unto us, thou Christ, Who is he that smote thee?"

A caviling criticism would demand: Why ask of the Christ to *prophesy* to those in His presence? And the obscurity would be damaging, were it not for an additional sentence in Luke, who records the same circumstance. "*And when they had blindfolded him*, they struck him on the face, and asked him, saying, Prophesy, Who is it that smote thee?"[272] The fact that Jesus was blindfolded, which is told by Luke, explains the use of the word "prophesy" by Matthew, which would otherwise be absurd.

Again, Matt. xiii. 2: "And great multitudes were gathered together with him, so that he went into the ship, and sat." Here, the definite article points to a particular ship which Matthew fails to mention. But Mark comes to his aid and clearly explains the statement: "And he spake to his disciples, that a small vessel should wait upon him because of the multitude, lest they should throng him." These two passages taken together identify the ship.

Again, John vi. 5: "When Jesus lifted up his eyes, and saw a great company come to him, he saith unto Philip, Whence shall we buy bread that these may eat?" This is one of the only two places in the Gospel where Jesus addressed this Apostle. But why ask Philip instead of one of the others? Two other passages, one from John and one from Luke, furnish an explanation. In John i. 44 we read that "Philip was of Bethsaida." In Luke ix. 10 we learn that the scene of the event, the miracle of feeding the five thousand, was "a desert place belonging to the city called Bethsaida." The reason, then, for addressing Philip, instead of one of the other Apostles, is clear. Bethsaida was the home of Philip; and he would naturally, therefore, be more familiar with the location of the bread shops than the others. In John vi., where the question is asked, neither the place of the feeding nor the apostle questioned is even remotely connected with the city of Bethsaida; and in Luke the account of the miracle says nothing of Philip or the question put to him. But when the passages are connected the striking coincidence appears, and the explanation is complete.

Again, John xviii. 10: "Then Simon Peter, having a sword, drew it and smote the high priest's servant, and cut off his right ear. The servant's name was Malchus." It has been objected that there is nowhere an account of the arrest or punishment of Peter for this assault and resistance to armed authority; and that, therefore, there was no such occurrence. A passage from Luke explains the failure to arrest. "And Jesus answered and said, Suffer ye thus far, and he touched his ear and healed him."[273] The healing of the ear explains why no arrest followed; for, if charges had been made, there would have been no evidence of the gravity of the offense. Indeed, witnesses against Peter would have been completely confounded and humiliated by the result of the miracle; and might have been driven from court as malicous accusers. Then, the failure to arrest is a silent corroboration of the statement that the event occurred and that the miracle was performed.

Under the third heading, of the "confirmation of logic or reason," a single instance will suffice.

John xx. 4: "And the other disciple did outrun Peter and came first to the sepulchre." The "other disciple" was St. John, who is generally conceded to have been the youngest of the Apostles. And St. Peter, we may judge from John xxi. 18, was already past the meridian of life. What could be more natural than that the younger man should outrun the older and arrive first at the sepulchre? What better proof could be expected of the fact of the existence of that sweetness and modesty in youth which respects old age, and that endeared John to Jesus above all others, than we have here, where the younger man awaits the arrival of the older before beginning to explore the deserted tomb?

Examples similar to these might be multipled at length, since the Gospel histories are filled with them; but those above mentioned are deemed sufficient to illustrate the theory of corroboration. The instances of internal confirmation in the New Testament narratives are especially convincing. They are arguments and proofs in the nature of undesigned coincidences which, from the very nature of the case, shut out all possibility of collusion or fraud. In most cases they are expressed in a single phrase and represent an isolated thought corroborative of some other elsewhere expressed. Though small, detached, and fragmentary, like particles of dynamite, they operate with resistless force when collected and combined.

Once more attention is called to the fact that these discrepancies negative completely the idea that the Gospel writers were conspirators, bent upon the common purpose of deceiving mankind by publishing a false history to the world. Nothing could be more absurd than to suppose that men conspiring to perpetrate a fraud, would neglect a fundamental principle underlying all successful conspiracy; that is, the creation and maintenance of a due and reasonable consistency between the words and deeds of the conspirators in formulating plans for carrying out the common purpose. Then, if there was no previous concert, the fact that four men, writing at different times and places, concurred in framing substantially the same history, is one of the strongest proofs of the credibility of the writers and the truthfulness of their narratives. And on this point the testimony of a very great writer may be quoted: that "in a number of concurrent testimonies, where there has been no previous concert, there is a probability distinct from that which may be termed the sum of the probabilities resulting from the testimonies of the witnesses; a probability which would remain, even though the witnesses were of such a character as to merit no faith at all. This probability arises from the concurrence itself. That such a concurrence should spring from chance is as one to infinite; that is, in other words, morally impossible. If, therefore, concert be excluded, there remains no cause but the reality of the fact."[274]

Apply the theory of probability, arising from concurrent testimonies, where there has been no previous concert, to the case of the Evangelists, and we are at once convinced that they were truthful and that their histories are true.

(4) Let us now consider the *conformity of the testimony of the Evangelists with human experience*. This is the fourth legal test of the credibility of witnesses prescribed by Starkie.

The conformity of testimony with experience is one of the most potent and universally applied tests of the credibility of witnesses. And it may be remarked that its application is not confined to judicial proceedings or to courts of law. It requires no professional attainments to make it effective. The blacksmith and carpenter, as well as the judge and jury, employ it in every mental operation where the statements of others are submitted to analysis and investigation. A new theory being proposed, the correctness of which is questioned, the test of experience is at once applied. If it is not in harmony with what we have seen and heard and felt, we usually reject it; or, at least, doubt it. If an explorer should return from the Arctic regions and tell us that he had seen oranges, such as we import from Florida, growing on trees near the North Pole, we would not believe him. Neither would we credit the statement of a traveler from South America that he had seen Polar bears browsing on the banks of the Amazon. These representations would be utterly inconsistent with what we know to be the essential conditions of orange culture, and with the well-known habits and climatic nature of the Polar bear. An ancient document, purporting to date from the time of Washington and the Revolution, and containing recitals about railways, telegraphs, telephones, and electric lights, would be recognized at once as spurious, because our own experience as well as facts of history would tell us that there were no such things in the days of Washington and the American Revolution. These are simple illustrations of the application of the test of experience in the mental processes of weighing and sifting the testimony of others.

Now, no serious objection to the credibility of the Gospel writers has been made under the test of the conformity of their statements with experience, except in the matter of miracles. It is generally admitted, even by skeptics, that the facts stated in the New Testament narratives might have happened in the due course of nature and in harmony with human experience, except where miracles are related.

A few skeptics have declared that a miracle is an impossibility and that the Evangelists were either deceivers or deceived when they wrote their accounts of the miraculous performances of the Christ; and that, whether deceivers or deceived, they are unworthy of belief. The great antagonist of the theory of miracles among those who assert their impossibility is Spinoza, who has thus written: "A miracle, whether contrary to or above nature, is a sheer absurdity. Nothing happens in nature which does not follow from its laws; these laws extend to all which enters the Divine mind; and, lastly, nature proceeds in a fixed and changeless course — whence it follows that the word 'miracle' can only be understood in relation to the opinions of mankind, and signifies nothing more than an event, a phenomenon, the cause of which cannot be explained by another familiar instance. . . . I might say, indeed, that a miracle was *that,* the cause of which cannot be explained by our *natural understanding from the known principles of natural things.*"

The radical antagonism of Spinoza to the doctrine of miracles, as taught in the New Testament scriptures, was the legitimate offspring of his peculiar philosophy. He was a pantheist and identified God with nature. He did not believe in a personal God, separate from and superior to nature. He repudiated the theory of a spiritual kingdom having a spiritual sovereign to whom earth and nature are subject and obedient. Therefore, every manifestation of power which he could not identify with a natural force he believed was unreal, if not actually deceptive and fraudulent; since he could not imagine anything superior to nature that could have created the phenomenon. His denial of miracles was, then, really nothing less than a denial of the existence of a personal God who spoke the earth into being in the very beginning; and has since, with a watchful paternal eye, followed its movements and controlled its destiny.

The question of miracles is really a matter of faith and not a problem of science. It is impossible to either prove or disprove the nature of a miracle by physical demonstration. In other words, it is impossible to analyze a miracle from the standpoint of chemistry or physics. The performance of a miracle, nevertheless, may be proved by ordinary human testimony, as any other event may be proved. We may testify to the fact without being able to understand or to demonstrate the cause.

Those who believe that there are distinct spiritual as well as physical forces in the universe; that there is somewhere an omniscient and omnipotent Spiritual Being who has but to will the creation of a planet or the destruction of matter in order to accomplish the result desired, can easily believe in the exercise of miraculous power. Those who believe the Bible account of the creation, that God said in the beginning, "Let there be light: and there was light" — such persons find no difficulty in believing that Jesus converted water into wine or caused the lame to walk, if they believe that He was this same God "manifest in the flesh." A divinity who, in the morning of creation, spoke something out of nothing, would certainly not be impotent to restore life to Lazarus or sight to the blind Bartimeus.

The trouble with the philosophy of Spinoza is that his own high priestess — Nature — seems to be constantly working miracles under his own definition; and miracles, too, that very closely resemble the wonders said to have been wrought by the Christ. Milk is taken into the stomach, subjected to various processes of digestion, is then thrown into the blood and finally becomes flesh and bone. The ultimate step in this process of transformation is unknown and, perhaps, unknowable to scientists. No deeper mystery is suggested by the New Testament scriptures. The conversion of water into wine is no stranger, no more incomprehensible than the transformation of milk into flesh and bone. It may be admitted that the chemical elements are the same throughout in one process and different in the other. Nevertheless, the results of both are perfectly described by Spinoza's definition, "that a miracle was *that*, the case of which cannot be explained by our *natural understanding from the known principles of natural things.*"

It may be truthfully remarked that nature is everywhere and at all times working wonders in harmony with and parallel to the miracles wrought by the spiritual forces of the universe. God's sovereign miracle may be described as the changing of a man, with all his sins and imperfections, into a winged spirit, thus fitting him to leave the coarse and vulgar earth for life among the stars. Nature, in her feeble way, tries to imitate the wonder by transforming the caterpillar into a butterfly, thus fitting it to leave the dunghill for life among the flowers.

Spinoza insists that miracles are impossible because "nature proceeds in a fixed and changeless course." But is this really true? Are the laws of nature invariably uniform? Does not nature seem at times tired of uniformity and resolved to rise to liberty by the creation of what we call a miracle, or more vulgarly, a "freak"? Moving in what Spinoza is pleased to call a "fixed and changeless course," nature ordinarily provides a chicken with two legs and a snake with one head. But what about chickens with three legs and snakes with two heads, such as are frequently seen? Was nature moving in a fixed and changeless course when these things were created? Could Spinoza have explained such phenomena by his "natural understanding from the known principles of natural things"? Would he have contented himself with calling them natural "accidents" or "freaks"? Nevertheless, they are miracles under his definition; and the entire subject must be discussed and debated with reference to some standard or definition of a miracle. If nature occasionally, in moments of sportiveness or digression, upsets her own laws and creates what we call "freaks," why is it unreasonable to suppose that the great God who created nature should not, at times, temporarily suspend the laws which He has made for the government of the universe, or even devote them to strange and novel purposes in the creation of those noble phenomena which we call miracles?

Other skeptics, like Renan, do not deny the possibility of miracles, but simply content themselves with asserting that there is no sufficient proof that such things ever happened. They thus repudiate the testimony of the Evangelists in this regard. "It is not," says Renan, "then, in the name of this or that philosophy, but in the name of universal experience, that we banish miracle from history. We do say that up to this time a miracle has never been proved." Then the Breton biographer and philosopher gives us his idea of the tests that should be made in order to furnish adequate proof that a miracle has been performed. "If tomorrow," he says, "a thaumaturgus presents himself with credentials sufficiently important to be discussed and announces himself as able, say, to raise the dead, what would be done? A commission composed of physiologists, physicists, chemists, persons accustomed to historical criticism would be named. This commission would choose a corpse, would assure itself that the death was real, would select a room in which the experiment should be made, would arrange the whole system of precautions, so as to leave no chance of doubt. If, under such conditions, the resurrection were effected, a probability almost equal to certainty would be established. As, however, it ought to be possible always to repeat an experiment — to do over again that which has been done once; and as, in the order of miracle, there can be no question of ease or difficulty, the thaumaturgus would be invited to reproduce his marvelous act under other circumstances, upon other corpses, in another place. If the miracle should succeed each time, two things would be proved: first, that supernatural events happen in the world; second, that the power of producing them belongs or is delegated to certain persons. But who does not see that no miracle ever took place under these conditions? But that always hitherto the thaumaturgus has chosen the subject of the experiment, chosen the spot, chosen the public?"[275]

This is an extract from the celebrated "Life of Jesus" by Renan, and is intended to demolish the Gospel account of the miracles of the Christ. It is not too much to say that the great skeptic has failed to exhibit his usual fairness in argument. He has indirectly compared Jesus to a thaumaturgus, and has inferentially stated that in the performance of His miracles He "chose the subject of his experiment, chose the spot, chose the public." Every student of New Testament history knows that this is not true of the facts and circumstances surrounding the performance of miracles by Christ. It is true that vulgar curiosity and caviling incredulity were not gratified by the presence of specially summoned "physiologists, physicists, and chemists." But it is equally true that such persons were not prevented from being present; that there was no attempt at secrecy or concealment; and that no subject of experiment, particular spot, or special audience was ever chosen. The New Testament miracles were wrought, as a general thing, under the open sky, in the street, by the wayside, on the mountain slope, and in the presence of many people, both friends and enemies of Jesus. There was no searching or advertising for subjects for experiment. Far from choosing the subject, the spot, and the public, Jesus exercised His miraculous powers upon those who came voluntarily to Him suffering with some dreadful malady and asking to be cured. In some instances, the case of affliction was of long standing and well known to the community. The healing was done publicly and witnessed by many people.

Renan suggests that the thaumaturgus mentioned in his illustration would be required to repeat his performance in the matter of raising the dead before he would be fully believed. This reminds us that Jesus wrought many miracles. More than forty are recorded in the Gospel narratives; and in the closing verse of St. John, there is a strong intimation that He performed many that were never recorded. These, it is respectfully submitted, were amply sufficient to demonstrate His miraculous powers.

Whatever form infidelity may assume in its antagonism to the doctrine of miracles, it will be found that the central idea is that such things are not founded in experience; and that this test of credibility fails in the case of the Gospel writers, because they knowingly recorded impossible events. It would be idle to attempt to depreciate the value of this particular test; but it must be observed that nothing is more fallacious, unless properly defined and limited. It must be remembered that the experience of one man, nation, or generation is not necessarily that of another man, nation, or generation. The exact mechanical processes employed by the Egyptians in raising the pyramids are as much as mystery to modern scientists as a Marconigram would be to a savage of New Guinea. The Orient and the Occident present to each other almost miraculous forms of diversity in manners, habits, and customs, in modes of thought and life. "The Frenchman says, 'I am the best dyer in Europe: nobody can equal me, and nobody can surpass Lyons.' Yet in Cashmere, where the girls make shawls worth $30,000, they will show him three hundred distinct colors, which he not only cannot make, but cannot even distinguish." Sir Walter Scott, in his "Tales of the Crusaders," thrillingly describes a meeting between the Turkish Saladin and the English Richard Coeur-de-Lion. Saladin asked Richard to give him an exhibition of his marvelous strength. The Norman monarch picked up an iron bar from the floor of the tent and severed it. The Mahometan crusader was amazed. Richard then asked him what he could do. Saladin replied that he could not pull iron apart like that, but that he could do something equally as wonderful. Thereupon, he took an eider-down pillow from the sofa, and drew his keen, Damascus-tempered blade across it, which caused it to fall into two pieces. Richard cried in astonishment: "This is the black art; it is magic; it is the devil: you cannot cut that which has no resistance!" Here Occidental strength and Oriental magic met and wrought seeming miracles in the presence of each other. In his great lecture on "The Lost Arts," Wendell Phillips says that one George Thompson told him that he saw a man in Calcutta throw a handful of floss silk into the air, and that a Hindoo severed it into pieces with his saber. A Western swordsman could not do this.

Objectors to miracles frequently ask why they are not performed to-day, why we never see them. To which reply may be made that, under Spinoza's definition, miracles are being wrought every day not only by nature, but by man. Why call Edison "the magician" and "the wizard," unless the public believes this? But is it any argument against the miracles of Jesus that similar ones are not seen to-day? Have things not been done in the past that will never be repeated? We have referred to the pyramids of Egypt and to the lost art involved in their construction. A further illustration may be found in the origin of man. One of two theories is undoubtedly true: that the first man and woman came into the world without being born; or that man and woman are the products of evolution from lower orders of animals. No other theories have ever been advanced as to the origin of the human race. Now, it is certain that modern generations have never experienced either of these things, for all the human beings of to-day were undoubtedly born of other human beings, and it is certain that the process of evolution stopped long ago, since men and women were as perfect physically and mentally four thousand years ago as they are to-day. In other words, the processes which originated man are things of the past, since we have no Garden of Eden experiences to-day, nor is there any universal metamorphosis of monkeys going on. Therefore, to argue that the miracles of Jesus did not happen, because we do not see such things to-day, is to deny the undoubted occurrences of history and developments of human life, because such occurrences and developments are no longer familiar to us and our generation.

To denounce everything as false that we have not individually seen, heard, and felt, would be to limit most painfully the range of the mental vision. The intellectual horizon would not be greatly extended should we join with our own the experience of others that we have seen and known. Much information is reported by telegraphic despatch and many things are told us by travelers that we should accept as true; although such matters may have no relation to what we have ever seen or heard. Else, we should be as foolish as the king of Siam who rejected the story of the Dutch ambassador, that in Holland water was frequently frozen into a solid mass. In the warm climate of the East Indian tropics the king had never seen water so congealed and, therefore, he refused to believe that such a thing had ever happened anywhere.

Experience is a most logical and reasonable test if it is sufficiently extended to touch all the material phases of the subject under investigation. It is a most dangerous one if we insist upon judging the material and spiritual universe, with its infinite variety of forms and changes, by the limited experience of a simple and isolated life, or by the particular standards of any one age or race. A progressive civilization, under such an application of the test, would be impossible, since each generation of men would have to begin *de novo*, and be restricted to the results of its own experience. The enforcement of such a doctrine would prevent, furthermore, the acceptance of the truths of nature discovered by inventive genius or developed by physical or chemical research, until such truths had become matters of universal experience. Every man would then be in the position of the incredulous citizen, who, having been told that a message had been sent by wire from Baltimore to Washington announcing the nomination of James K. Polk for the presidency, refused to believe in telegraphic messages until he could be at both ends of the line at once. The art of telegraphy was a reality, nevertheless, in spite of his incredulity and inexperience. The American savages who first beheld the ships of Columbus are said to have regarded them as huge birds from heaven and to have refused to believe that they were boats, because, in their experience, they had never seen such immense canoes with wings. Herodotus tells us of some daring sailors who crept along the coast of Africa beyond the limits usually visited at that time. They came back home with a wonderful account of their trip and told the story that they had actually reached a country where their shadows fell toward the south at midday. They were not believed, and their report was rejected with scorn and incredulity by the inhabitants of the Mediterranean coasts, because their only experience was that a man's shadow always pointed toward the north; and they did not believe it possible that shadows could be cast otherwise. But the report of the sailors was true, nevertheless.[276]

These simple illustrations teach us that beings other than ourselves have had experiences which are not only different from any that we have ever had, but are also either temporarily or permanently beyond our comprehension. And the moral of this truth, when applied to the statements of the Evangelists regarding miracles, is that the fortunate subjects and witnesses of the miraculous powers of Jesus might have had experiences which we have never had and that we cannot now clearly comprehend.

(5) In the fifth and last place, as to the *coincidence of their testimony with collateral circumstances*.

This is the chief test of credibility in all those cases where the witness, whose testimony has been reduced to writing, is dead, absent, or insane. Under such circumstances it is impossible to apply what may be termed personal tests on cross-examination; that is, to develop the impeaching or corroborating features of bias, prejudice, and personal demeanor to the same extent as when the witness is still living and testifies orally. When a written narrative is all that we have, its reliability can only be ascertained by a close inspection of its parts, comparing them with each other, and then with collateral and contemporaneous facts and circumstances. The value of this test cannot be over-estimated, and Greenleaf has stated very fully and concisely the basis upon which it rests. "Every event," he says, "which actually transpires, has its appropriate relation and place in the vast complication of circumstances of which the affairs of men consist; it owes its origin to the events which have preceded it, is intimately connected with all others which occur at the same time and place, and often with those of remote regions, and in its turn gives birth to numberless others which succeed. In all this almost inconceivable contexture and seeming discord, there is perfect harmony; and while the fact which really happened tallies exactly with every other contemporaneous incident related to it in the remotest degree, it is not possible for the wit of man to invent a story, which, if closely compared with the actual occurrences of the same time and place, may not be shown to be false."[277]

This principle offers a wide field to the skill of the cross-examiner, and enables him frequently to elicit truth or establish falsehood when all other tests have failed. It is a principle also perfectly well known to the perjurer and to the suborner of witnesses. Multiplicity of details is studiously avoided by the false witness, who dreads particularity and feels that safety lies in confining his testimony as nearly as possible to a single fact, whose attendant facts and circumstances are few and simple. When the witness is too ignorant to understand the principle and appreciate the danger, his attorney, if he consents to dishonor his profession and pollute the waters of justice with corrupt testimony, may be depended upon to administer proper warning. The witness will be told to know as few things and to remember as little as possible concerning matters about which he has not been previously instructed. The result will be that his testimony, especially in matters in which he is compelled by the court to testify, will be hesitating, restrained, unequal, and unnatural. He will be served at every turn by a most convenient memory which will enable him to forget many important and to remember many unimportant facts and circumstances. He will betray a painful hesitancy in the matter of committing himself upon any particular point upon which he has not been already drilled. The truthful witness, on the other hand, is usually candid, ingenuous, and copious in his statements. He shows a willingness to answer all questions, even those involving the minutest details, and seems totally indifferent to the question of verification or contradiction. Thes texture of his testimony is, therefore, equal, natural, and unrestrained.

Now these latter characteristics mark every page of the New Testament histories. The Gospel writers wrote with the utmost freedom, and recorded in detail and with the utmost particularity, the manners, customs, habits, and historic facts contemporaneous with their lives. The naturalness and ingenuousness of their writings are simply marvelous. There is nowhere any evidence of an attempt to conceal, patch up, or reconcile. No introductory exclamations or subsequent explanations which usually characterize false testimony appear anywhere in their writings. They were seemingly absolutely indifferent to whether they were believed or not. Their narratives seem to say: These are records of truth; and if the world rejects them it rejects the facts of history. Such candor and assurance are always overwhelmingly impressive; and in every forum of debate are regarded as unmistakable signs of truth.

The Evangelists, it must be assumed, were fully aware of the danger of too great particularity in the matter of false testimony, and would have hesitated to commit themselves on so many points if their statements had been untrue. We have already noted the opinion of Professor Holtzmann, of

Heidelberg, that the Synoptic Gospels were committed to writing between the years 60 and 80 of our era. At that time it is certain that there were still living many persons who were familiar with the events in the life and teachings of the Savior, as well as with the numerous other facts and circumstances related by the sacred writers. St. Paul, in I Cor. xv. 6, speaks of five hundred brethren to whom the risen Jesus appeared at one time; and he adds, *"of whom the greater part remain unto this present, but some are fallen asleep."* And it must be remembered that this particular group of two hundred and fifty or more were certainly not the only persons then living who had a distinct remembrance of the Master, His teachings, and His miracles. Many who had been healed by Him, children who had sat upon His knee and been blessed by Him, and many members of the Pharisaic party and of the Sadducean aristocracy who had persecuted Him and had then slain Him, were doubtless still living and had a lively recollection of the events of the ministry of the Nazarene. Such persons were in a position to disprove from their personal knowledge false statements made by the Evangelists. A consciousness of this fact would have been, within itself, a strong inducement to tell the truth.

But not only are the Gospels not contradicted by contemporaneous writers; they are also not impeached or disproved by later scientific research and historical investigation. And at this point we come to make a direct application of the test of the coincidence of their testimony with collateral and contemporaneous history. For this purpose, as a matter of illustration, only facts in profane history corroborative of the circumstances attending the trial and crucifixion of the Master will be cited.

In the first place, the Evangelists tell us that Pontius Pilate sat in judgment on the Christ. Both Josephus and Tacitus tell us that Pilate was governor of Judea at that time.[278]

In John xviii. 31 we read: "Then said Pilate unto them, Take ye him, and judge him according to your law. The Jews therefore said unto him, *It is not lawful for us to put any man to death.*" From many profane historians, ancient and modern, we learn that the power of life and death had been taken from the Jews and vested in the Roman governor.[279]

In John xix. 16, 17 occurs this passage: "And they took Jesus, and led him away; and he, *bearing his cross,* went forth." This corroborative sentence is found in Plutarch: "Every kind of wickedness produces its own particular torment; just as every malefactor, when he is brought forth to execution, *carries his own cross.*"[280]

In Matthew xxvii. 26 we read: "When he had scourged Jesus, he delivered him to be crucified." That scourging was a preliminary to crucifixion among the Romans is attested by many ancient writers, among whom may be mentioned Josephus and Livy. The following passages are taken from Josephus:

> Whom, having *first scourged with whips,* he crucified.[281]
> Being *beaten,* they were crucified opposite to the citadel.[282]
> He was burned alive, *having been first beaten.*[283]

From Livy, a single sentence will suffice:

> All were led out, *beaten with rods,* and beheaded.[284]

In John xix. 19, 20 we read: "And Pilate wrote a title and put it on the cross; and it was written in Hebrew, and Greek, and Latin." That it was a custom among the Romans to affix the accusation against the criminal to the instrument of his punishment appears from several ancient writers, among them Suetonius and Dion Cassius. In Suetonius occurs this sentence. "He exposed the father of the family to the dogs, with this *title,* 'A gladiator, impious in speech.' "[285] And in Dion Cassius occurs the following: "Having led him through the midst of the court or assembly, *with a writing signifying the cause of his death, and afterwards crucifying him.*"[286]

And finally, we read in John xix. 32: "Then came the soldiers and *brake the legs* of the first, and of the other which was crucified with him." By an edict of Constantine, the punishment of crucifixion was abolished. Speaking in commendation of this edict, a celebrated heathen writer mentions the circumstances of *breaking the legs.* "He was pious to such a degree," says this writer, "that he was the first to set aside that very ancient punishment, the cross, with the *breaking of legs*.[287]

If we leave the narrow circle of facts attendant upon the trial and crucifixion of Jesus with its corroborative features of contemporary history, and consider the Gospel narratives as a whole, we shall find that they are confirmed and corroborated by the facts and teachings of universal history and experience. An examination of these narratives will also reveal a divine element in them which furnishes conclusive proof of their truthfulness and reliability. A discussion of the divine or spiritual element in the Gospel histories would be foreign to the purpose of this treatise. The closing pages of Part I will be devoted to a consideration of the human element in the New Testament narratives. This will be nothing more than an elaboration of the fifth legal test of credibility mentioned by Starkie.

By the human or historical element of credibility in the Gospel histories is meant that likeness or resemblance in matters of representation of fact to other matters of representation of fact which we find recorded in secular histories of standard authority whose statements we are accustomed to accept as true. The relations of historic facts to each other, and the connections and coincidences of things known or believed to be true with still others sought to be proved, form a fundamental ground of belief, and are, therefore, reliable modes of proof. The most casual perusal of the New Testament narratives suggests certain striking resemblances between the events therein narrated and well-known historical occurrences related by secular historians whose statements are implicitly believed. Let us draw a few parallels and call attention to a few of these resemblances.

Describing the anguish of the Savior in the Garden, St. Luke says: "And being in an agony, He prayed more earnestly: And his sweat was as it were great drops of blood falling down to the ground."[288]

This strange phenomenon of the "bloody sweat" has been of such rare occurrence in the history of the world that its happening in Gethsemane has been frequently denied. The account of it has been ascribed to the overwrought imagination of the third Evangelist in recording the errors of tradition. And yet similar cases are well authenticated in the works of secular writers. Tissot reports a case of "a sailor who was so alarmed by a storm, that through fear he fell down, and his face sweated blood which, during the whole continuance of the storm, returned like ordinary sweat, as fast as it was wiped away."[289] Schenck cites the case of "a nun who fell into the hands of soldiers; and, on seeing herself encompassed with swords and daggers threatening instant death, was so terrified and agitated that she discharged blood from every part of her body, and died of hemorrhage in the sight of her assailants."[290] Writing of the death of Charles IX of France, Voltaire says: "The disease which carried him off is very uncommon; his blood flowed from all his pores. This malady, of which there are some examples, is the result either of excessive fear, furious passion, or of a violent and melancholic temperament."[291] The same event is thus graphically described by the old French historian, De Mezeray: "After the vigor of his youth and the energy of his courage had long struggled against his disease, he was at length reduced by it to his bed at the castle of Vincennes, about the 8th of May, 1574. During the last two weeks of his life his constitution made strange efforts. He was affected with spasms and convulsions of extreme violence. He tossed and agitated himself continually and his blood gushed from all the outlets of his body, even from the pores of his skin, so that on one occasion he was found bathed in a bloody sweat."[292]

If the sailor, the nun, and the king of France were afflicted with the "bloody sweat," why should it seem incredible that the man Jesus, the carpenter of Nazareth, should have been similarly afflicted? If Tissot, Schenck, and Voltaire are to be believed, why should we refuse to believe St. Luke? If St. Luke told the truth in this regard, why should we doubt his statements concerning other matters relating to the life, death, and resurrection of the Son of God? Does not Voltaire, the most brilliant and powerful skeptic that ever lived, corroborate in this particular the biographer of the Christ?

Let us pass to another instance of resemblance and corroboration. While describing the crucifixion, St. John wrote the following: "But one of the soldiers with a spear pierced his side, and forthwith came there out *blood and water*."[293] Early skeptical criticism denied the account of the flowing of blood and water from the side of the Savior because, in the first place, the other Evangelists did not mention the circumstance; and, in the second place, it was an unscientific fact stated. But modern medical science has very cleverly demonstrated that Jesus, according to the Gospel accounts, died of rupture of the heart. About the middle of the last century, a celebrated English physician and surgeon, Dr. Stroud, wrote a treatise entitled, "Physical Cause of the Death of Christ." In this book, he proved very clearly that cardiac rupture was the immediate cause of the death of Jesus on the cross. Many arguments were adduced to establish this fact. Among others, it was urged that the shortness of time during which the sufferer remained upon the cross and His loud cry just before "He gave up the ghost," tended to prove that a broken heart was the cause of the death of the Man of Sorrows. But the strongest proof, according to the author of this work, was the fact that blood and water flowed from the dead man when a spear was thrust into His side. This, says Dr. Stroud, has happened frequently when the heart was suddenly and violently perforated after death from cardiac rupture. Within a few hours after death from this cause, he says, the blood frequently separates into its constituent parts or essential elements: *crassamentum*, a soft clotted substance of deep-red color, and *serum*, a pale, watery liquid — popularly called blood and water, which will flow out separately, if the pericardium and heart be violently torn or punctured. In this treatise numerous medical authorities are cited and the finished work is indorsed by several of the most famous physicians and surgeons of England.

It is very probable that St. John did not know the physical cause of the strange flow of blood and water from the side of Jesus. It seems that he was afraid that he would not be believed; for, in the following verse, he was careful to tell the world that he himself had personally seen it. "And he that *saw it* bare record, and his record is true: And he knoweth that he saith true that ye might believe."[294]

Here again modern medical science has corroborated, in the matter of the flowing of blood and water from the side of Jesus, the simple narrative of the gentle and loving Evangelist.

Still another illustration of resemblance, coincidence, and corroboration is furnished by the incident of the arrest of Jesus in the Garden. St. John says: "As soon, then, as he had said unto them, I am he, they went backward and fell to the ground."[295]

This is only one of several cases mentioned in history where ordinary men have been dazed and paralyzed in the presence of illustrious men against whom they were designing evil. When a Gallic trooper was sent by Sulla to Minturnae to put Marius to death, the old Roman lion, his great eyes flashing fire, arose and advanced toward the slave, who fled in utter terror from the place, exclaiming, "I cannot kill Caius Marius!"[296]

Again, we learn from St. Matthew that at the moment of the arrest in the Garden, "all the disciples forsook him and fled."

This is no isolated case of cowardice and desertion. It is merely an illustration of a universal truth: that the multitude will follow blindly and adore insanely the hero or prophet in his hour of triumph and coronation, but will desert and destroy him at the moment of his humiliation and crucifixion.

Note the burning of Savonarola. The patriot-priest of the Florentine Republic believed himself inspired of God; his heroic life and martyr death seemed to justify his claim. From the pulpit of St. Mark's he became the herald and evangel of the Reformation, and his devoted followers hung upon his words as if inspiration clothed them with messages from the skies. And yet when a wicked Inquisition had nailed him to the cross and fagots were flaming about him, this same multitude who adored him, now reviled him and jeered and mocked his martyrdom.

Note the career of Napoleon. When the sun of Austerlitz rose upon the world the whole French nation grew delirious with love and homage for their emperor, who was once a subaltern of Corsica. But when the Allies entered Paris after the battle of Leipsic, this same French nation repudiated their imperial idol, cast down his images, canceled his decrees, and united with all Europe in demanding his eternal banishment from France. The voyage to Elba followed. But the historic melodrama of popular fidelity and fickleness was not yet completely played. When this same Napoleon, a few months later, escaped from his islet prison in the Mediterranean and landed on the shores of France, this same French nation again grew delirious, welcomed the royal exile with open arms, showered him with his eagles, and almost smothered him with kisses. A hundred days passed. On the frightful field of Waterloo, "Chance and Fate combined to wreck the fortunes of their former king." Again the fickle French multitude heaped execrations upon their fallen monarch, declared the Napoleonic dynasty at an end and welcomed with acclamations of joy the return of the exiled Bourbon Louis XVIII.

And when the Evangelist wrote these words: "All the disciples forsook him and fled," he simply gave expression to a form of truth which all history reflects and corroborates.

Again, the parallels and resemblances of sacred and profane history do not seem to stop with mere narratives of facts. Secular history seems to have produced at time characters in the exact likeness of those in sacred history. The resemblance is often so striking as to create astonishment. For instance, who was St. Peter but Marshal Ney by anticipation? Peter was the leader of the Apostolic Twelve; Ney was the chief of the Twelve Marshals of Napoleon. Peter was impulsive and impetuous; so was Ney. Peter was the first to speak and act in all the emergencies of the Apostolic ministry; Ney, so Dumas tells us, was always impatient to open the battle and lead the first charge. Peter was probably the last to leave the garden in which the great tragedy of his Master had begun; Ney was the last to leave the horrors of a Russian winter in which the beginning of the end of the career of his monarch was plainly seen. Peter denied Jesus; Ney repudiated Napoleon, and even offered to bring him, at the time of his escape from Elba, in a cage to Louis XVIII. Peter was afterwards crucified for his devotion to Jesus whom he had denied; Ney was afterwards shot for loyalty to Napoleon whom he had once repudiated.

The examples heretofore given involve the idea of comparison and are based upon resemblance. These illustrations could be greatly extended, but it is believed that enough has been said in this connection. However, in closing this brief discussion of the human element in the sacred writings as evidence by the coincidences and resemblances of their narratives to those of profane history, slight mention may be made of another test of truth which may be applied to the histories of the Evangelists. This test is not derived from a comparison which is focused upon any particular group of historic facts. It springs from an instantaneously recognized and inseparable connection between the statements made by the Gospel writers and the experience of the human race. A single illustration will suffice to elucidate this point. When Jesus was nailed upon the cross, the sad and pathetic spectacle was presented of the absence of the Apostolic band, with the exception of St. John, who was the only Apostle present at the crucifixion. The male members of the following of the Nazarene did not sustain and soothe their Master in the supreme moment of His anguish. But the women of His company were with Him to the end. Mary, his mother, Mary Magdalene, Mary, the wife of Cleophas, Salome, the mother of St. John the Evangelist, and others, doubtless among "the women that followed him from Galilee," ministered to His sufferings and consoled Him with their presence. They were the last to cling to His cross and the first to greet Him on the morning of the third day; for when the resurrection morn dawned upon the world, these same women were seen hastening toward the sepulchre bearing spices — fragrant offerings of deathless love. What a contrast between the loyalty and devotion of the women and the fickle, faltering adherence of the men who attended the footsteps of the Man of Sorrows in His last days! One of His

Apostles denied Him, another betrayed Him, and all, excepting one, deserted Him in His death struggle. His countrymen crucified Him ignominiously. But "not one woman mentioned in the New Testament ever lifted her voice against the Son of God."

This revelation from the sacred pages of the devotion of woman is reflected in universal history and experience. It is needless to give examples. Suffice it to say that when Matthew, Mark, Luke, and John tell us of this devotion, we simply answer: yes, this has been ever true in all countries and in every age. We have learned it not only from history but from our own experience in all the affairs of life, extending from the cradle to the grave. The night of sorrow never grows so dark that a mother's love will not irradiate the gloom. The criminal guilt of a wayward son can never become so black that her arms will not be found about him. If we pass from loving loyalty to the individual, to patriotic devotion to the causes of the nations, woman's fidelity is still undying. The women of France are said to have paid the German war debt. The message of the Spartan mother to her soldier son is too well known to be repeated. When the legions of Scipio engirdled the walls of Carthage and desperation seized the inhabitants of the Punic city, Carthaginian women cut their long black hair to furnish bowstrings to the Carthaginian archers. Illustrations might be multiplied; but these will suffice to show that Mary and Martha and Salome, the women of the Gospels, are simply types of the consecrated women of the world.

When we come to summarize, we are led to declare that if the Gospel historians be not worthy of belief we are without foundation for rational faith in the secular annals of the human race. No other literature bears historic scrutiny so well as the New Testament biographies. Not by a single chain, but by three great chains can we link our Bible of to-day with the Apostolic Bible. The great manuscripts: the Vatican, the Alexandrian, and the Sinaitic, dating from the middle of the fourth and fifth centuries, must have been copies of originals, or at least of first copies. The Bible is complete in these manuscripts to-day.

The Versions, translations of the original Scriptures from the language in which they were first written into other languages, form a perfect connection between the days of the Apostles and our own. The Vulgate, the celebrated Latin version of St. Jerome, was completed A.D. 385. In making this translation the great scholar has himself said that he used "ancient (Greek) copies." Manuscripts that were ancient, A.D. 385, must have been the original writings, or, at least, first copies. The Vulgate, then, is alone a perfect historic connection between the Bible that we read to-day and that studied by the first Christians.

Again, the Writings of the Church Fathers furnish a chain, without a single missing link, between the Bible of this generation and that of the first generation of the followers of the Christ. It has been truthfully said that if all the Bibles in the world were destroyed an almost perfect Bible could be reconstructed from quotations from these writings, so numerous and so exact are they. Beginning with Barnabas and Clement, companions of St. Paul, and coming down through the ages, there is not a single generation in which some prince or potentate of the Church has not left convincing evidence in writing that the Books of the Old and New Testament which we read to-day are identical with those read by the first propagators of our faith. The chain of proof forged from the Writings of the early Fathers is made up of a hundred links, each perfect within itself and yet relinked and welded with a hundred others that make each and all doubly strong. If these various testimonies, the Manuscripts, the Versions, and the Writings of the Church Fathers, be taken, not singly, but collectively, in support and corroboration of each other, we have, then, not merely a chain but rather a huge spiritual cable of many wires, stretching across the great sea of time and linking our Bible of to-day inseparably with that of the Apostolic Age.

If it be objected that these various writings might have been and probably were corrupted in coming down to us through the centuries, reply may be made that the facts of history repel such suggestions. As Mr. Greenleaf has suggested, the jealousy of opposing sects presesrved them from forgery and mutilation. Besides these sects, it may be added, there were, even in the earliest times, open and avowed infidels who assaulted the cardinal tenets of the Christian faith and made the Gospel histories the targets for their attacks. They, too, would have detected and denounced any attempt from any source to corrupt these writings.

Another and final, and probably the most cogent reason for the remarkable preservation of the books of the Bible, is the reverential care bestowed upon them by their custodians in every age. It is difficult for the modern world to fully appreciate the meaning and extent of this reverence and care. Before the age of printing, it must be remembered, the masses of the people could not and did not possess Bibles. In the Middle Ages it required a small fortune to own a single copy. The extreme scarcity enhanced not only the commercial value but added to the awful sanctity that attached to the precious volume; on the principle that the person of a king becomes more sacred and mysterious when least seen in public. Synagogues and monasteries were, for many centuries, the sole repositories of the Holy Books, and the deliberate mutilation of any portion of the Bible would have been regarded like the blaspheming of the Deity or the desecration of a shrine. These considerations alone are sufficient reason why the Holy Scriptures have come down to us uncorrupted and unimpaired.

These various considerations are the logical basis of that rule of law laid down by Mr. Greenleaf, under which the Gospel histories would be admitted into a modern court of law in a modern judicial proceeding.

Under legal tests laid down by Starkie, we have seen that the Evangelists should be believed, because: (1) They were honest and sincere, that is, they believed that they were telling the truth; (2) they were undoubtedly men of good intelligence and were eyewitnesses of the facts narrated by them in the New Testament histories; (3) they were independent historians, who wrote at different times and places and, in all essential details, fully corroborate each other; (4) excepting in the matter of miracles, which skepticism has never been able to fully disprove, their testimony is in full conformity with human experience; (5) their testimony coincides fully and accurately with all the collateral, social, historical, and religious circumstances of their time, as well as with the teachings and experience of universal history in every age.

Having received from antiquity an uncorrupted message, born of truth, we have, it is believed, a perfect record of fact with which to discuss the trial of Jesus.

(Chandler, Walter M., *The Trial of Jesus*, Vol. 1, New York: The Empire Publishing Co., 1908, pp. 12-70.)

Notes

Complete bibliographical data is shown in the case of the first reference to a particular source. Subsequent references to the same source list only the author's name and title of book or article.

1. Thomas Arnold, *Sermons on the Christian Life — Its Hopes, Its Fears, and Its Close*, p. 324.
2. Brooke F. Westcott, *The Gospel of the Resurrection*, 4th ed., London, n.p., 1879, pp. 4-6.
3. Paul L. Maier, *Independent Press-Telegram*, Long Beach, Calif., April 21, 1973, p. A-10.
4. Linton H. Irwin, *A Lawyer Examines the Bible*, Grand Rapids, Mich., Baker Book House, 1943, p. 14.
5. Wilbur Smith, *Therefore Stand*, Grand Rapids, Mich., Baker Book House, 1965, pp. 425, 584.
6. Val Grieve, *Verdict on the Empty Tomb*, London, Church Pastoral Aid Society, 1976, p. 26.
7. C.S. Lewis, *Surprised by Joy*, London, Geoffrey Bles, 1955, pp. 211, 215, 223.
8. Matthew 16:21; Mark 8:31; Luke 9:22 (paraphrased).
9. Mark 8:31.
10. John 2:19-21.
11. I Corinthians 15:13-17.
12. Anderson, J.N.D., *Christianity: The Witness of History*, copyright Tyndale Press 1970, Inter-Varsity Press, Downer's Grove, Ill., p. 13.
13. Romans 1:4.
14. Newbigin, James Edward Leslie, *The Finalty of Christ*, Richmond, John Knox Press, 1969, p. 62.
15. John 8:32.
16. Matthew 22:37.
17. I Peter 3:15.
18. Burkholder, Lawrence, "A Dialogue on Christ's Resurrection," *Christianity Today*, Vol. XII, April 12, 1968, p. 6.

19. Ibid.

20. Ibid, p. 7.

21. Clark Pinnock, "The Tombstone That Trembled," *Christianity Today*, Vol. XII, April 12, 1968, p. 8.

22. Ibid, p. 10.

23. John Warwick Montgomery, *Where Is History Going?* Minneapolis, Bethany Fellowship, 1967, p. 71.

24. William Neil, *The Rediscovery of the Bible*, p. 33.

25. Vincent Taylor, *The Formation of the Gospel Tradition*, ltd. 2nd ed., London, MacMillan and Co., 1935, p. 135.

26. II Peter 1:16.

27. I Timothy 1:4.

28. John 9:32.

29. Acts 17:16-34.

30. *The New Encyclopedia Britannica*, Vol. VIII, Micropaedia, 22nd ed., Chicago, H. Hemingway Pub., 1981, p. 985.

31. James B. Conant, *Science and Common Sense*, New Haven, Yale Univ. Press, 1951, p. 25.

32. *The Basic Dictionary of Science*, New York, MacMillan and Co., 1965, p. 404.

33. *The Harper Encyclopedia of Science*, James R. Newman, ed., New York, Harper & Row, 1967, p. 1048.

34. Acts 1:3.

35. Wolfhart Pannenberg, "A Dialogue on Christ's Resurrection," *Christianity Today*, Vol. XII, April 12, 1968, p. 10.

36. Ronald Sider, "A Case for Easter," *His*, April 1972, pp. 27-31.

37. Ethelbert Stauffer, *Jesus and His Story*, transl. by Dorothea M. Barton, New York, Knopf, 1960, p. 17.

38. Philip Schaff, *History of the Christian Church*, Vol. 1, New York, Charles Scribner's Sons, 1882, p. 175.

39. F.F. Bruce, *The New Testament Documents: Are They Reliable?* 5th ed., Downer's Grove, Ill., Inter-Varsity Press, 1960, p. 119.

40. *Federal Rules of Evidence*, St. Paul, West Publishing Co., 1979, Rule 901 (b) (8). Also see McCormick's *Handbook of the Law of Evidence*, Edward W. Cleary, ed., St. Paul, West Publishing Co., 1972, p. 560.

41. John Warwick Montgomery, "Legal Reasoning and Christian Apologetics," *The Law Above the Law*, Oak Park, Ill., Christian Legal Society, 1975, pp. 88, 89.

42. William F. Albright, *Recent Discoveries in Biblical Lands*, New York, Funk & Wagnalls, 1955, p. 136.

43. John A.T. Robinson, *Time*, March 21, 1977, p. 95.

44. Frederick G. Kenyon, *The Bible and Archaeology*, New York, Harper & Row, 1940, p. 288.

45. F.F. Bruce, *The New Testament Documents: Are They Reliable?* p. 15.

46. Paul L. Maier, *First Easter*, New York, Harper & Row, 1973, p. 122.

47. William F. Albright, *From the Stone Age to Christianity*, 2nd ed., Baltimore, Johns Hopkins Press, 1946, pp. 297, 298.

48. Millar Burrows, *What Mean These Stones?* New York, Meridian Books, 1956, p. 52.

49. Ibid, p. 2.

50. Howard Vos, *Can I Trust My Bible?* Chicago, Moody Press, 1963, p. 176.

51. Louis Gottschalk, *Understanding History*, 2nd ed., New York, Knopf, 1969, pp. 150, 161, 168.

52. II Peter 1:16.

53. Acts 1:1-3.

54. Luke 1:1-3.

55. Elizabeth S. Loftus, "The Eyewitness on Trial," *Trials*, Vol. 16, No. 10, Oct. 1980, pp. 30-35. Also Buckhout, "Eyewitness Testimony," *Scientific American*, Dec. 1974, pp. 23-31.

56. Ibid.

57. McCormick's *Handbook of the Law of Evidence*, Edward W. Cleary, ed., St. Paul, West Publishing Co., 1972, pp. 586, 587.

58. *Federal Rules of Evidence*, Rule 801 and 802.

59. John Warwick Montgomery, "Legal Reasoning and Christian Apologetics," pp. 88, 89.

60. Matthew 28:1-7.

61. Matthew 28:9,10.

62. Matthew 28:16-20.

63. Luke 24:24.

64. John 20:24-29.
65. *Federal Rules of Evidence*, Rule 803(5).
66. Acts 2:22.
67. McCormick's *Handbook of the Law of Evidence*, p. 43.
68. Justice Ruffin, in *State v. Morriss*, 84, N.C. 764.
69. John Warwick Montgomery, "Legal Reasoning and Christian Apologetics," pp. 88, 89.
70. F.F. Bruce, *The New Testament Documents: Are They Reliable?* pp. 44-46.
71. Louis Gottschalk, *Understanding History*, p. 151.
72. Acts 1:1.
73. Stan Gundry, *An Investigation of the Fundamental Assumption of Form Criticism*, thesis presented to Dept. of N.T. Language and Lit., Talbot Theol. Seminary, June, 1963, p. 45.
74. Louis Gottschalk, *Understanding History*, p. 168.
75. Ibid.
76. William M. Ramsay, *The Bearing of Recent Discovery on the Trustworthiness of the New Testament*, London, Hodder & Stoughton, 1915, p. 222.
77. William M. Ramsay, *St. Paul the Traveller and the Roman Citizen*, Grand Rapids, Mich., Baker Book House, 1962.
78. Acts 18:12.
79. Acts 28:7.
80. Acts 17:6.
81. Acts 14:6.
82. Luke 3:1.
83. E.M. Blaiklock, *The Acts of the Apostles*, Grand Rapids, Mich., Wm. B. Eerdmans Publ. Co., 1959, p. 89.
84. F.F. Bruce, "Archaeological Confirmation of the New Testament," *Revelation and the Bible*, Carl Henry, ed., Grand Rapids, Mich., Baker Book House, 1969, p. 331.
85. F.F. Bruce, *The New Testament Documents: Are They Reliable?* p. 90.
86. Philo, *Logatio and Gaium* 38.
87. John 18:13.
88. Matthew 26:57.
89. Matthew 26:59.
90. Matthew 27:2.
91. Luke 23:7.

92. Luke 23:11-25.
93. Matthew 27:11.
94. Haim Cohn, "Reflections on the Trial," *Judaism*, Vol. 20, 1971, p. 11; also *The Trial of Jesus*, Joseph Blinzler.
95. Justin, *Digest* 48, 4, 1:48, 4, 11.
96. Haim Cohn, "Reflections on the Trial," p. 11.
97. Robert M. Grant, "The Trial of Jesus in the Light of History," *Judaism*, Vol. 20, 1971, p. 39.
98. Solomon Zeitlin, "The Crucifixion of Jesus Re-examined," *Jewish Quarterly Review*, Vol. 31, 1940-41, p. 366.
99. Ibid.
100. David Flusser, "A Literary Approach to the Trial of Jesus," *Judaism*, Vol. 20, 1971, p. 30.
101. Ibid.
102. Paul L. Maier, *First Easter*, p. 24.
103. Solomon Zeitlin, "The Crucifixion of Jesus Re-examined," p. 335.
104. Ibid.
105. Matthew 27:26.
106. Cicero, *V in Verrem*, 64.
107. Will Durant, *Caesar and Christ*, New York, Simon & Schuster, 1944, p. 572.
108. Flavius Josephus, *De Bello Judaico*, 7.202, 203.
109. Luke 23:2.
110. Ernst Bammel, "Crucifixion as a Punishment in Palestine," *The Trial of Jesus*, Naperville, Ill., Alex R. Allenson, Inc., 1920, p. 162.
111. Deuteronomy 21:23.
112. C. Truman Davis, "The Crucifixion of Jesus," *Arizona Medicine*, March 1965, p. 185.
113. Eusebius, "The Epistle of the Church in Smyrna," *Trials and Crucifixion of Christ*, A.P. Stout, ed., Cincinnati, Standard Publishing, 1886.
114. Will Durant, *Caesar and Christ*, p. 572.
115. Pierre Barbet, *A Doctor at Calvary*, New York, P.S. Kennedy & Sons, 1953, p. 44.
116. J.W. Hewitt, "The Use of Nails in the Crucifixion," *Harvard Theological Review*, Vol. 25, 1932, pp. 29-45.
117. N. Haas, "Anthropological Observations on the Skeletal

Remains from Giv' at ha-Mivtar," *Israel Exploration Journal*, Vol. 20, 1970, p. 39.

118. Ibid, p. 42.
119. John 19:32, 33.
120. N. Haas, "Anthropological Observations on the Skeletal Remain from Giv' at ha-Mivtar," p. 57.
121. Ibid, p. 58.
122. C. Truman Davis, "The Crucifixion of Jesus," *Arizona Medicine*, p. 186.
123. Ibid, p. 185, 186.
124. Stuart Bergsma, "Did Jesus Die of a Broken Heart?" *The Calvin Forum*, March 1948, p. 165.
125. Ibid.
126. Ibid.
127. Will Durant, *Caesar and Christ*, p. 572.
128. Ibid, p. 573.
129. Paul L. Maier, *First Easter*, p. 112.
130. V. Tzaferis, "Jewish Tombs at and Near Giv' at ha-Mivtar, Jerusalem," *Israel Exploration Journal*, Vol. 20, 1970, p. 30.
131. Robert Willis, "Architectural History of the Holy Sepulchre," *Holy City*, ed. George Williams, London, John W. Parker Publ., Vol. II, 1849.
132. Seder Nezikin, "Sanhedrin 46a," *The Babylonian Talmud*, London, The Sancino Press, 1935, p. 304.
133. M. Shabbath 23.5.
134. A.P. Bender, "Beliefs, Rites, and Customs of the Jews, Connected With Death, Burial, and Mourning," *The Jewish Quarterly Review*, Vol. VII, 1895, pp. 259, 260.
135. Flavius Josephus, *Antiquities of the Jews*, Vol. 3, Chap. 8, Sec. 3.
136. A.P. Bender, "Beliefs, Rites, and Customs of the Jews, Connected With Death, Burial, and Mourning," *The Jewish Quarterly Review*, p. 261.
137. Ibid.
138. John Chrysostom, *Homilies of St. John*, Grand Rapids, Mich., Wm. B. Eerdmans, reprint 1969, p. 321.
139. Matthew 27:60.
140. Mark 16:1-4.
141. Matthew 27:63.

142. Maier, Paul L., *First Easter*, p. 111.
143. Matthew 28:11.
144. T.G. Tucker, *Life in the Roman World of Nero and St. Paul*, St. Martin's St., London, Macmillan & Co., Ltd., 1910, pp. 340-342.
145. Polybius VI. 37, 38.
146. T.G. Tucker, *Life in the Roman World of Nero and St. Paul*, p. 342.
147. Matthew 27:66.
148. Daniel 6:17.
149. Paul L. Maier, *First Easter*, p. 119.
150. Ibid, pp. 118, 119.
151. Paul L. Maier, "The Empty Tomb as History," *Christianity Today*, Vol. XIX, March 28, 1975, p. 5.
152. Ibid.
153. Matthew 28:11-15.
154. Acts 5:34-42.
155. Ronald Sider, "A Case for Easter," p. 29.
156. Conversation with Josh McDowell, author, January 1981.
157. Paul L. Maier, "The Empty Tomb as History," *Christianity Today*, p. 6.
158. George Currie, *The Military Discipline of the Romans from the Founding of the City to the Close of the Republic*, abstract of thesis published under auspices of Graduate Council of Indiana Univ., 1928, pp. 41-43.
159. Bill White, *A Thing Incredible*, 1944, Israel, Yanetz Ltd., 1976.
160. I Corinthians 15.
161. Yamauchi, Edwin, "Easter—Myth, Hallucination, or History?" *Christianity Today*, March 29, 1974, p. 13.
162. I Corinthians 15:6.
163. Tenney, Merrill C., "The Resurrection of Jesus Christ," *Prophecy in the Making*, Carl Henry, ed., Carol Stream, Ill., Creation House, 1971, p. 59.
164. Acts 8:1, 9:1, 2; Philippians 3:5, 6.
165. Acts 9:3-6.
166. John 7:5.
167. I Corinthians 15:7.
168. Acts 6:7.

The Resurrection Factor

169. Paul L. Maier, *First Easter*, p. 98.

170. J.N.D. Anderson, *Christianity: The Witness of History*, p. 105.

171. Philip Schaff, *History of the Christian Church*, p. 175.

172. Charles Alford Guignebert, *Jesus*, New York, Univ. Book, Inc., 1956, p. 500.

173. Kirsopp Lake, *The Historical Evidence for the Resurrection of Jesus Christ*, New York, G.P. Putnam's Sons, 1907, pp. 250-253.

174. Matthew 28:6; Mark 16:6; Luke 24:6.

175. Paul L. Maier, *First Easter*, p. 122.

176. William F. Albright, *From the Stone Age to Christianity*, pp. 297, 298.

177. J.N.D. Anderson, "The Resurrection of Jesus Christ," *Christianity Today*, March 29, 1968, p. 6.

178. J.W. Drane, "Some Ideas of Resurrection in the New Testament Period," *Tyndale Bulletin*, Vol. 24, 1973, p. 103.

179. Ibid, p. 101.

180. Luke 24:39.

181. Matthew 28:9.

182. Theodore R. Sarbin and Joseph B. Juhaz, "The Social Contact of Hallucinations," *Hallucinations: Behavior, Experience and Theory*, R.K. Siegel and L.J. West, eds., New York, John Wiley & Sons, p. 242, 1975.

183. Ibid.

184. Ibid, p. 243.

185. Ibid.

186. L.E. Hinsie and R.J. Campbell, "Hallucination," *Psychiatric Dictionary*, p. 333.

187. J.P. Brady, "The Veridicality of Hypnotic, Visual Hallucinations," *Origin and Mechanisms of Hallucinations*, Wolfram Keup, ed., New York, Plenum Press, 1970, p. 37.

188. Johannes Weiss, *Earliest Christianity: A History of the Period A.D. 30-150*, Vol. 1, ed. & transl. by Fredrick C. Grant, New York, Harper Torchbooks, reprinted 1959, p. 287.

189. Theodore R. Sarbin and Joseph B. Juhaz, "The Social Context of Hallucinations," *Hallucinations: Behavior, Experience and Theory*, p. 242.

190. Luke 24:41, 42; John 21:13.

191. Luke 24:39, 40; John 20:27.

192. See page 71.
193. Paul Little, *Know Why You Believe*, Wheaton, Scripture Press, 1967, pp. 68, 69.
194. Acts 5:17-42.
195. Matthew 27:62-66.
196. Bill White, *A Thing Incredible*, p. 9.
197. George Raymond Beasley-Murray, *Christ Is Alive*, London, Lutterworth Press, 1947, p. 63.
198. Paul Althaus, *Die Wahrheit des Kirchlichen Osterglaubens*, p. 22.
199. Paul L. Maier, *First Easter*, p. 120.
200. Matthew 28:11-15.
201. George Currie, *The Military Discipline of the Romans from the Founding of the City to the Close of the Republic*, pp. 41-43.
202. Matthew 26:56.
203. Edward Gibbons, *The History of the Decline and Fall of the Roman Empire*, Chicago, William Benton, Publ., reprinted 1952, p. 179.
204. Simon Greenleaf, *An Examination of the Testimony of the Four Evangelists by the Rules of Evidence Administered in the Courts of Justice*, Grand Rapids, Mich., Baker Book House, 1965; reprint of 1874 ed., New York, J. Cockroft & Co., p. 29.
205. J.N.D. Anderson, *Christianity: The Witness of History*, p. 92.
206. David F. Strauss, *Das Leben Jesu*, Darnstadt: Wissenschaftliche Buchgesellschaft, 1835, reprint 1969, p. 289.
207. Joseph Klausner, *Jesus of Nazareth*, New York, Macmillan & Co., 1925, p. 414.
208. Acts 5:33-42.
209. John Warwick Montgomery, *History and Christianity*, p. 35.
210. E. Le Camus, *The Life of Christ*, Vol. III, New York, Cathedral Library Assn., 1908, p. 486.
211. David Friedrick Strauss, *The Life of Jesus for the People*, Vol. 1, 2nd ed., London, William & Norgate, 1879, p. 412.
212. *Saturday Review*, December 3, 1966, p. 43.
213. *Newsweek*, August 8, 1966, p. 51.
214. J.N.D. Anderson, "Resurrection of Jesus Christ," p. 9.
215. Paul L. Maier, *First Easter*, p. 113.
216. McCormick's *Handbook of the Law of Evidence*, pp. 435-437. See also Val Grieve, *Verdict on the Empty Tomb*, p. 20.
217. Val Grieve, *Verdict on the Empty Tomb*, p. 20.

218. Acts 2:41.
219. J.N.D. Anderson, "Resurrection of Jesus Christ," p. 9.
220. Daniel Fuller, *Easter Faith and Histsory*, Grand Rapids, Mich., Wm. B. Eerdmans, 1965, p. 259.
221. John 7:1-5.
222. John 14:6; 15:5; 10:11.
223. Acts 1:13, 14.
224. James 1.
225. Flavius Josephus, *Antiquities of the Jews*, Vol. 3, BK 20, Chap. 9, Sec. 1.
226. I Corinthians 15:7.
227. Matthew 26:56; Mark 14:50.
228. John 18:15-27; Mark 14:66-72.
229. John 20:19.
230. I Corinthians 15:5-7.
231. Acts 8:1-3; 9:1, 2; 22:3-5.
232. Acts 9:22.
233. I Corinthians 15:8; Acts 9:3-22; 22:6-21.
234. Robert Grant, *Historical Introduction to the New Testament*, New York, Harper & Row, 1963, p. 302.
235. Simon Greenleaf, *An Examination of the Testimony of the Four Evangelists by the Rules of Evidence Administered in the Courts of Justice*, p. 29.
236. George Eldon Ladd, *The New Testament and Criticism*, Grand Rapids, Mich., Wm. B. Eerdmans, 1967, p. 188.
237. I Corinthians 15:3.
238. I Corinthians 15:19-26.
239. John 10:10.
240. John 5:15-18; 10:25-33; for further claims to deity see *More Than a Carpenter*, pp. 9-24.
241. Isaiah 1:18.
242. Matthew 12:40.
243. Matthew 12:40.
244. Mark 8:31; Matthew 16:21.
245. John 2:19-22.
246. Matthew 27:63.
247. I Samuel 30:12, 13.
248. Genesis 42:17.
249. Matthew 12:40.

250. *Mishnah*, Third Tractate, "B. Pesachim," p. 4a.
251. *Mishnah*, Tractate "J. Shabbath," Chapter IX, Par. 3.
252. Arthur C. Custance, *The Resurrection of Jesus Christ*, Doorway Papers, #46, Brookville, 1971, p. 17.
253. John 10:30: "I and my Father are one."
254. Matt. 9:9.
255. Col. 4:14: "Luke, the beloved physician."
256. Matt. 26:70-72.
257. Matt. 26:46-50.
258. Matt. 26:56.
259. Matt. 14:28-31.
260. Mark 10:35-42; Matt. 20:20-25.
261. Matt. 11:2,3.
262. Mark 3:21.
263. Luke 4:28,29.
264. Mark 14:51,52.
265. "Intro. Vie de Jesus."
266. Luke 1:2,3.
267. "Die synoptischen Evangelien," pp. 412-14.
268. Marcus Dods, "The Bible, Its Origin and Nature," p. 184.
269. An opposite doctrine seems to be taught in Luke 12:11, 12; 24:48,49.
270. "Evidences of Christianity," p. 319.
271. Matt. 14:12-20; Mark 6:34-43; Luke 9:12-17; John 6:5-13.
272. Luke 22:64.
273. Luke 22:51.
274. Campbell's "Philosophy of Rhetoric," c.v.b. 1, Part III, p. 125.
275. "Intro. Vie de Jesus," p. 62.
276. D.L. Moody, "Sermon on the Resurrection of Jesus."
277. See also "Starkie on Evidence," pp. 496-99.
278. "Ant.," XVII. 3, 1.
279. See authorities cited in "The Brief."
280. "De iis qui sero puniuntur," p. 554.
281. P. 1080, edit. 45.
282. P. 1247, edit. 24, Huds.
283. P. 1327, edit. 43.
284. "Productique omnes, virgisque caesi, ac securi percussi," Lib. XI. c. 5.

285. Domit. Cap. X. "Patremfamilias meanibus objecit, cum hoc *titulo*, Impie loctus, parmularius."

286. Book LIV.

287. "Aur. Vict. Ces.," Cap. XLI. "Eo pius, ut etiam vetus veterrimumque supplicium, patibulum, et cruribus suffringendis, primus removerit." Also see Paley's "Evidences of Christianity," pp. 266-68.

288. Luke 22:44.

289. Tissot, "Traite des Nerfs," pp. 279, 280.

290. Joannes Schenck a Grafenberg, "Observ. Medic.," Lib. III. p. 458.

291. Voltaire, "Oeuvres completes," vol. xviii. pp. 531, 532.

292. De Mezeray, "Histoire de France," vol. iii. p. 306.

293. John 19:34.

294. John 19:35.

295. John 18:6.

296. "Encyc. Brit.," vol. xv. p. 550.